CYCLISTS' ROUTE ATLAS

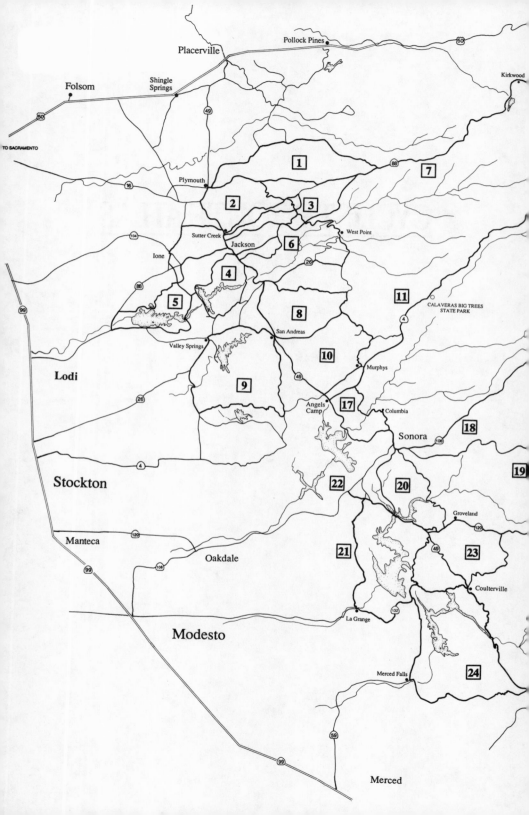

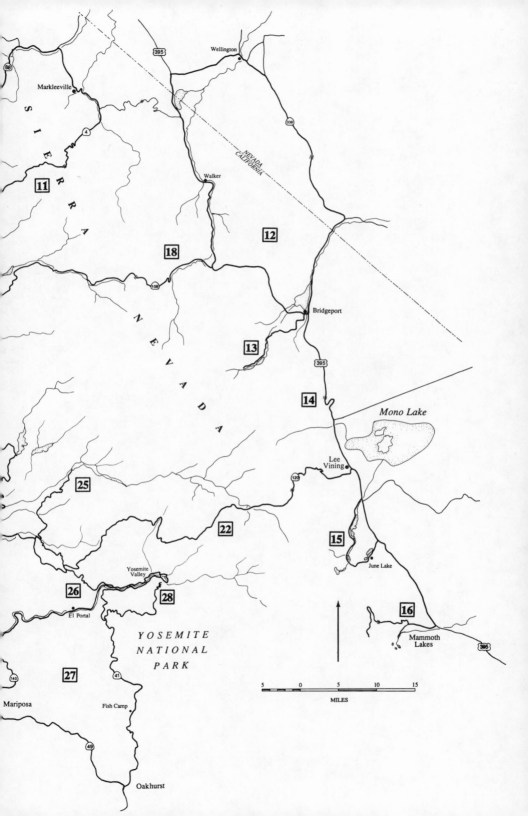

HEYDAY BOOKS

CYCLISTS' ROUTE ATLAS

A GUIDE TO

The Gold Country & High Sierra/South

RANDALL GRAY BRAUN

Printed in the United States of America.

10   9   8   7   6   5   4   3   2   1

Published by Heyday Books
Box 9145
Berkeley, California 94709

ISBN: 0-930588-29-0

Cover and interior photos: Randall Braun
Cover design: Nancy Austin and Sarah Levin
Interior design: Randall Braun
Editing and proofing: Elizabeth Weiss and Miriam Kaminsky

Cover photo: Highway 108, near Sonora Pass.

ACKNOWLEDGMENTS

This book is dedicated to my father and mother, whose unfailing support, both emotional and financial, made this book possible. They were there through some difficult times and I want them to know I am forever grateful. I would like to thank Larry Zulch, Bren Smith, and Walt Hays for their time and energies with the computer and I also want to thank John Padgett for his help rebuilding my measuring wheel. The Beyond War organization of Palo Alto deserves special recognition for allowing me to use their printer. I mustn't forget Ben, Kevin, and Serena for their mapping skills, and Beth too. And to all the others who lent support and encouragement when I needed it, thank you.

TABLE OF CONTENTS

INTRODUCTION

Welcome to the Southern Sierra Nevada mountains. Here you will find some of the most fantastic and beautiful country in the world. A previous guide in this series covered the Northern Sierra region. The southern area, also, is a region of lonely rolling hills, challenging mountain passes, colorful history, expansive valleys, idiosyncratic towns, beautiful weather, and sparkling rivers and lakes. A bicycle, unlike most forms of modern transportation, will transform a simple journey through this area into an adventure, a challenge, and a rich experience that you will never forget. With the help of this Route Atlas you can explore the Sierra with confidence, finding places away from the masses and hordes, choosing routes to suit your ability and interest. Believe it or not, some of the most scenic routes in this book are quite flat too.

Four distinct regions are covered in this guide: the lonely grass- and oak-dotted lower foothills; the Gold Country, with its rich and colorful history and well-preserved towns; the High Sierra, with snow-capped peaks, cold-rushing rivers, and warm alpine meadows; and the East Slope and deserts, with sage, pinyon pines, and boundless vistas. The routes are grouped according to the city or town from which they originate. The two routes that begin at Plymouth, for example, are presented together.

The beautiful Sierra Nevada is very popular as a vacation destination. This guide, with its clustering of routes, can help you plan a relatively unburdened cycling vacation. Rather than load down your beast with food and gear for a week, locate one of the marvelous inns or campgrounds, and base camp from there. This will free you to explore the region more fully while traveling light at whatever pace you choose. You can mix and match the routes for whatever type of terrain and length challenges you. You can cycle for days without seeing the same road more than once, unless you want to. And you'll never have to lug forty pounds of gear over a pass.

This guide will provide you with high-quality route information so you can plan trips in the High Sierra, Gold Country, or East Slope with assurance. Once you become familiar with the region, the possibilities for adventure are almost endless. While exploring and researching this guide, the Sierra, with her abundant beauty, has renewed my love and respect for this planet of ours. I hope it does the same for you.

SAFETY

One of the primary goals of this guide is to promote safe cycling. Now before I go one step further, I must state that cycling is a potentially dangerous activity and most cycling accidents can be attributed to pilot error. I also know experience, not a book, is the best teacher. But the Sierra presents hazards not commonly found elsewhere, and it would be irresponsible of me not to mention them.

• High altitude. Until you become acclimated, your physical and mental performance can be reduced due to the lower levels of oxygen.

• Sudden weather changes. It is possible to get both severe sunburn and hypothermia on the same ride.

• Road hazards. The potential for accident is increased on fast descents by debris in the road. This can take many forms, from rocks and potholes to pine cones and broken bottles. Logging trucks and motor homes present a real threat, especially on the miles of narrow shoulderless highways so common in the region. When descending on narrow roads, claim your space out from the right shoulder. The danger comes when a passing vehicle is forced to choose between hitting an oncoming vehicle or running you off the road. When a vehicle approaches from behind and you can see the road ahead is clear, move over and allow it to pass. It is also important to deal with these situations in a courteous manner and not be a lout.

Now that I've convinced you to vacation in Mexico, let me say that all these hazards can be greatly reduced if you do one thing: Use your head! First and foremost that means wearing an approved helmet. It also means planning your trip to avoid highly congested areas and times. Ride in a consistent, predictable manner, and obey the rules of the road, especially stop signs. By doing so, you are saying to other traffic, "you can trust me." Squirrely behavior makes other drivers and cyclists very nervous. Always ride within your ability to respond to any hazards and learn to expect them. Be sure to wear bright clothing and prepare for possible foul weather. Take proper care of your body by eating well and, especially drinking plenty of fluids. Dehydration is a major reason for riders not finishing long rides. Keep your machine in top condition and make sure you can handle roadside repairs and emergencies, or ride with someone who can. And don't bite off more than you can chew. Being prepared mentally, not just physically, for the route you select is more important than most cyclists realize. The purpose of cycling is to enjoy yourself and experience beauty, not to torture yourself and your friends. If you practice good habits whenever you ride, cycling can be a healthy and rewarding activity for many, many years.

TOTAL CLIMB

The "total climb" number at the beginning of each route description indicates the total feet climbed, not just the net gain. The elevation data was obtained with an aircraft altimeter during the route-measuring process. To decide how challenging a route might be, you must also consider total route distance, as well as the duration and rate of each climb. Most of the routes presented are loops, so the total climb is the same no matter which direction you travel. The one-way routes all begin at a lower elevation and end at a higher elevation, so the total climb figure would be much smaller if measured in the other direction. The total climb figures have much the same effect on the reader as the route profiles: trepidation. Keep in mind that most of these routes are long, averaging over 50 miles, and the area covered is mountainous. The majority of these routes, therefore, are beyond the ability of a novice cyclist. But you will soon discover, if you haven't already, that the more you ride, the shorter the miles become, the smaller the hills too. So remember, what appears impossible now will be an accomplishment some day soon.

AVERAGE PAVEMENT QUALITY

While measuring these routes, I discovered that the pavement quality was much higher than I anticipated. Therefore, I will not burden you with a pavement quality rating for each ride but will only mention it when it is noteworthy. Almost all the routes are an even mix of Grade One (smooth asphalt) and Grade Two (even, yet coarse pavement called "chip seal"). There are short stretches of Grade Three (rough, bumpy, and patched pavement with occasional open potholes) on some routes, and I will mention them as they occur. I am happy to report that there is no Grade Four pavement (dirt roads) included in this guide.

SHOULDER WIDTH

Because a shoulder can be the margin you need to navigate some of these busy highways safely, I will mention the shoulder width within the description so you will know what to expect. But you can assume that most of the lightly traveled back roads have no shoulder. I divided the possibilities into three types. No shoulder means nothing beyond the narrow white line along the edge of most roads and highways. A narrow shoulder is between 1 and 3 feet wide, beyond the white line. A wide shoulder is 3 feet or more in width. These are rare and don't last for many miles because they are expensive to build and maintain, especially in these rural counties with small budgets. In some rare cases, as in Yosemite Valley, there are designated bike lanes along the road and bike paths separate from the road.

MAP KEY

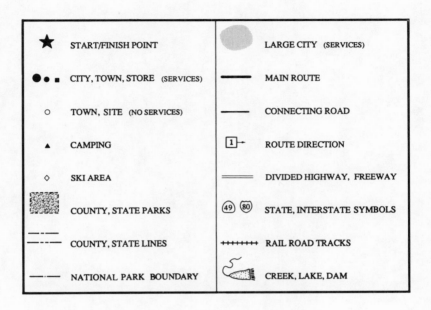

★ START/FINISH POINT	LARGE CITY (SERVICES)
●● ■ CITY, TOWN, STORE (SERVICES)	⎯⎯ MAIN ROUTE
○ TOWN, SITE (NO SERVICES)	⎯⎯ CONNECTING ROAD
▲ CAMPING	1 ⊢ ROUTE DIRECTION
◇ SKI AREA	═══ DIVIDED HIGHWAY, FREEWAY
COUNTY, STATE PARKS	49 80 STATE, INTERSTATE SYMBOLS
⎯ ⎯ ⎯ COUNTY, STATE LINES	+++++++ RAIL ROAD TRACKS
⎯·⎯ NATIONAL PARK BOUNDARY	CREEK, LAKE, DAM

PLYMOUTH

The first two routes begin at the sleepy little foothill town of Plymouth, located on Highway 49, thirty-five miles east of Sacramento via Highway 16. The routes start on busy Highway 49, but downtown Plymouth is to the west and has original false-front buildings with a shop or two. Warm summer days inevitably produce a lazy dog napping in the shade. Lodging is a bit scarce here but accommodations can be found in nearby Sutter Creek, Placerville, and Jackson. Excellent camp sites can be found near Pine Grove at Chaw-se Indian Grinding Rock State Historical Park.

This largely agricultural and grape growing region around Plymouth has many wonderful roads that will delight cyclists of all abilities. There are many small gold rush towns with lots to see and do throughout the area. As a rule, the roads west of Highway 49 are more gentle and rolling than those to the east. Traffic is often a factor in the gold country; take extra care when traveling on busy narrow-shouldered Highway 49. Highway 16 in Sacramento County is also very narrow and should be avoided when cycling to this area from Sacramento.

1 OMO RANCH

Starting Point: *Plymouth*
Distance: *53.8 miles*

Total Climb: *4,290 ft.*
Map: *Pages 10-11*

Grassy hillsides, vineyards, oak and cedar forests, and cool, shaded creeks mark this route. It is not as strenuous as the profile might suggest. Even though the climb is long, it's never very steep and the variety of country makes the miles fly by. The descent, on the other hand, is one of the best in this guide and shouldn't be missed.

Begin in Plymouth at the store on Highway 49 at Fiddletown Road. Travel east 5.7 miles to the hamlet of Fiddletown. The general store there is a rare vestige, with creaky, worn wooden floors and many subtle smells to transport you back in time. Continue ascending through oaks and pines passing Hale Road. Continue east, and a mile past a shady junction where a sign says "Volcano 6 Miles", you will find a roadside store where you can rest and refill your water bottles. The road narrows before the northeast turn on Highway 88. This highway is often busy, but after about three miles turn north on Omo Ranch Road and re-enter the lonely cedar, oak, and pine forest. Caution: 3.75 miles ahead there is a cattle guard that eats wheels and must be crossed with extreme care. The warning signs have a bad habit of getting shot full of holes and run over, so don't depend on them. Omo Ranch has a few ranch houses, a school, and an abandoned post office, but River Pines is 10.7 miles further down and has a store that sells a super sandwich and cold drinks. The remaining nine miles continue through vineyards and walnut groves before returning to Plymouth.

Novice cyclists might consider an easy loop from Plymouth to River Pines and back, or maybe Fiddletown and back. Enjoy.

2 HALE OF A ROAD

Starting Point: *Plymouth*
Distance: *39.3 miles*

Total Climb: *4,360 ft.*
Map: *Pages 10-11*

Yes, this is a hilly route, but if you're up to a few short, steep climbs, it's one of the prettiest, especially during the warm days of spring when the hills above Highway 49 are close to heavenly.

From the store on Highway 49 in Plymouth, head east to Fiddletown where the old store is open daily, 9-6. Turn south on Hale Road two miles beyond the store and climb through tall pines and cedar. There is a low water crossing at mile 10.5 and shortly beyond it, the road becomes bumpy (Grade Three) over to Shake Ridge Road. From Shake Ridge Road turn south on Charleston-Volcano Road. This road drops quickly, climbs, and drops again down to the wonderful little town of Volcano. Historic Volcano claims many firsts, including the first public library and the first literary society in California. Although there is nothing volcanic in Volcano, the town is otherwise very authentic. The store has a good restaurant, and ice cream is often sold from a shop next door. The little park across the street is a peaceful picnic spot. Pass the three-story hotel as you leave town south bound on Pine Grove-Volcano Road and be sure to stop and see the fascinating

Hale Road, looking east.

Indian village at Chaw-se Indian Grinding Rock State Historic Park. Turn west on Highway 88, pass through Pine Grove, and shortly thereafter turn west on Ridge Road across from the Beacon gas station. The delightful descent continues as you turn north on Highway 49 into bustling Sutter Creek. Climb a bit before you roll into Amador City and have some ice cream. Beyond Drytown, pass the Highway 16 junction, and continue north on Highway 49 back to Plymouth.

Even if you don't feel up to cycling to Volcano, be sure to drive up and spend a few hours there.

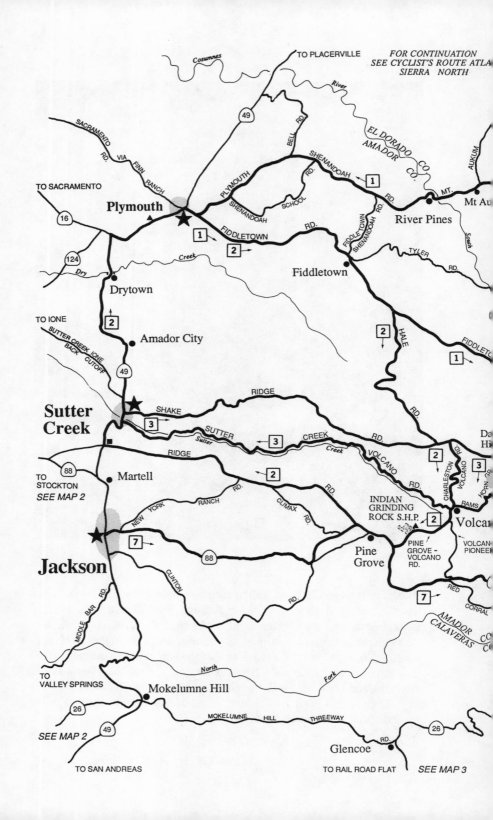

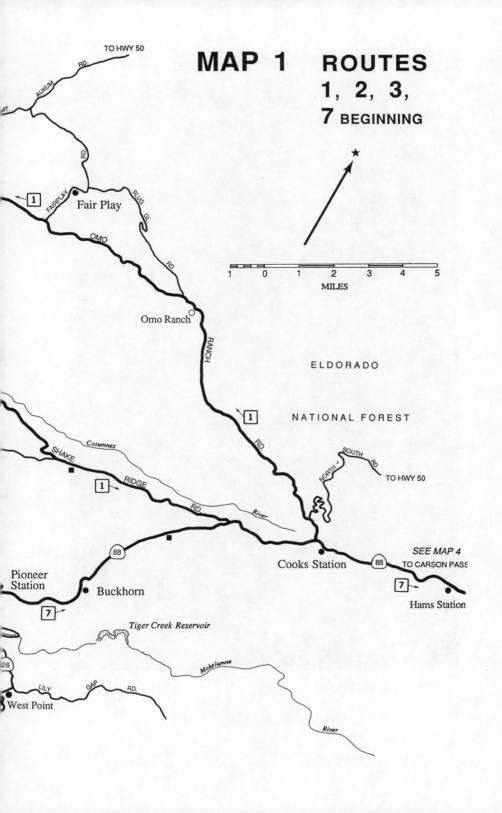

MAP 1   ROUTES 1, 2, 3, 7 BEGINNING

TO HWY 50

AUKUM RD.

MT.

RD.

1

FAIRPLAY

Fair Play

SLUG GL.

OMO

RD.

1   0   1   2   3   4   5

MILES

Omo Ranch

RANCH

ELDORADO

NATIONAL FOREST

RD.

1

Cosumnes

SHAKE

NORTH

SOUTH RD.

TO HWY 50

1

RIDGE

RD.

River

88

Cooks Station

88

SEE MAP 4
TO CARSON PASS

Pioneer
Station

7

Buckhorn

7

Hams Station

Tiger Creek Reservoir

26

Mokelumne

LILY

GAP   RD.

West Point

River

Shady picnic spot in Volcano.

SUTTER CREEK

Routes 3 through 7, which originate in Sutter Creek and Jackson, are so intertwined that you can start excellent trips from either location. The roads that travel through this region are delightful and varied enough to suit almost any requirement.

Sutter Creek has B&B's, restaurants, shops, historical sites, a picturesque Main Street, and a cool shady park for a picnic. Summer days are warm and the temperature often exceeds ninety degrees. Summer weekends are also the prime tourist season throughout the gold country, so if you choose to cycle on a summer weekend be sure to start early, carry plenty of water, and avoid Highway 49 as much as possible. Spring and fall are excellent choices for touring this region. The traffic has thinned, it's cooler, and the area is bursting with color. Winter days are often cold and damp, but sunny dry days are not uncommon. Call the Amador County Chamber of Commerce in Jackson for information on special events and lodging in the area.

3 DAFFODIL HILL

Starting Point: *Sutter Creek*
Distance: *28.2 miles*

Total Climb: *2,010 ft.*
Map: *Pages 10-11*

This route is a great intermediate tour that leads to one of my favorite towns in the region, Volcano. If you're a novice cyclist, you can shorten this route by riding the cool canyon along Sutter Creek to Volcano, where you can enjoy a hearty lunch and a nap in the park before heading back down along the creek. But you will miss one of the most colorful and unique places in the Sierra, Daffodil Hill. Tens of thousands of bulbs bloom on this hillside each April, and visitors stroll and picnic here while admiring the loving handiwork of the landowner.

From Sutter Creek at the post office, travel east on Gopher Flat Road, which becomes Shake Ridge Road beyond town. After 12.5 miles, turn south on Rams Horn Grade and pass Daffodil Hill and the

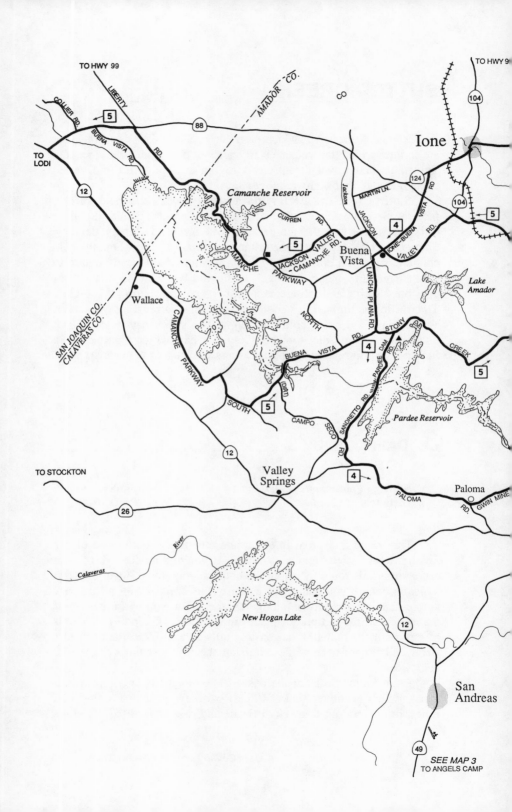

MAP 2 ROUTES 4, 5, 6.

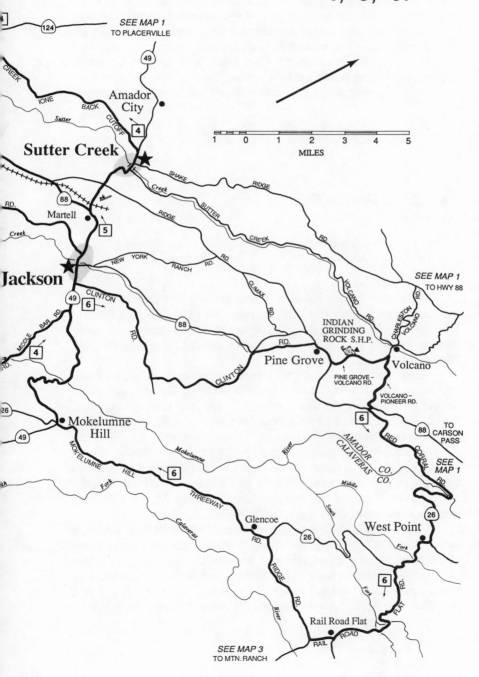

124

SEE MAP 1
TO PLACERVILLE

49

CREEK

IONE

BACK

CUTOFF

Sutter

Amador
City

4

Sutter Creek

1 0 1 2 3 4 5
MILES

88

Martell

RD.

Creek

SHAKE

Creek

RIDGE

RIDGE

SUTTER

CREEK

RD.

5

Jackson

49

6

CLINTON

RD.

NEW YORK

RANCH

RD.

88

CLIMAX

RD.

CLINTON

RD.

VOLCANO

RD.

SEE MAP 1
TO HWY 88

CHARLESTON

VOLCANO

RD.

INDIAN
GRINDING
ROCK S.H.P.

Pine Grove

Volcano

PINE GROVE -
VOLCANO RD.

4

MIDDLE

BAR

RD.

RD.

26

49

Mokelumne
Hill

MOKELUMNE

HILL

Mokelumne

Fork

6

THREEWAY

Calaveras

VOLCANO -
PIONEER RD.

6

RED

CORRAL

88

TO
CARSON
PASS

SEE
MAP 1

AMADOR

CALAVERAS

CO.

CO.

River

Middle

South

Fork

Glencoe

RD.

26

West Point

26

Fork

6

RIDGE

RD.

FLAT

RD.

River

Rail Road Flat

RAIL   ROAD

SEE MAP 3
TO MTN. RANCH

picnic area immediately on the left.   Rams Horn Grade is steep and windy so take it easy as you descend through an aromatic forest of tall pines and oaks.   Arrive in Volcano about three miles later, enter "downtown", and stop at the store and restaurant for lunch. The little park across the street makes a wonderful resting spot. The locals are very friendly as well as famous for their summer outdoor theater, which is sold out months in advance. After lunch, exit town to the south, pass the three-story hotel, and turn west on Sutter Creek-Volcano Road to be drawn delightfully along, beside the cool creek, back to where you began.

4 LET'S PARDEE

Starting Point: *Sutter Creek*
Distance: *39.2 miles*

Total Climb: *2,780 ft.*
Map: *Pages 14-15*

The rolling golden foothills of western Amador County provide the setting for a wonderful half-day loop that passes through historic Ione and Buena Vista, tours Pardee Reservoir, and continues south through the foothills before turning north through lonely Paloma and Highway 49.

From Main Street in Sutter Creek, travel north on Highway 49 and about a half mile out of town turn west on Sutter Creek High School Street, where the sign is often missing; then turn north on Ione Road, which becomes Sutter Creek Ione Back Cutoff. At the crest, begin the descent to Ione, an important stage stop during the gold rush. To get through Ione, follow Highway 124 south to W. Main Street, turn east, then immediately south on S. Church (still Hwy 124) across from the public restrooms. Continue down to veer southeast on Ione-Buena Vista Road. After crossing busy Highway 88, pass the clay mine that opened in 1864 and is still in operation today.

Continue on to Buena Vista, which has little more than a store, a saloon, some old buildings and many memories. Begin Lancha Plana Road there. Cross a bridge, veer east, and pass through vineyards before turning east at the stop sign onto Stony Creek Road . After .7 mile, turn south on Pardee Dam Road (the sign is often missing) and two miles later cross the narrow dam into Calaveras County. Turn east on

Looking east over Pardee Reservoir and dam.

Campo Seco Road, then north on Paloma Road. The country is mostly rolling grass- and oak-covered hills to this point. But Gwin Mine Road from Paloma descends through a steep wooded and shrub-filled canyon, passing the remains of what was Gwin Mine. Cross a green steel bridge over the languid Mokelumne River and climb out to Highway 49. Jackson is just over a mile north, and the historic old section of town is just east of the highway and worth a visit. Beyond Jackson, climb out to Martell and descend, still on busy Highway 49, to Sutter Creek.

JACKSON

Jackson, the Amador County seat, is a favorite of the central Gold Country. The well preserved, narrow Main Street has authentic old time shops, hotels, and restaurants. Be sure to give the little diner just north of the Safeway on Highway 49 a try. They open early and serve a mean stack of pancakes with O. J. and hash browns, guaranteed to fuel you for at least fifty miles. Parking is plentiful at Safeway or just north at the 24 hour city lot. For longer stays, see the police or the Chamber of Commerce. Weather is typical of the central Highway 49 region; pleasant and mostly dry in the spring and fall, hot in the summer, and above the valley fog in the winter. You can't be too cautious with the busy tourist traffic, especially on weekends; it's bad. Watch out for thirty foot rented motor homes pulling wide boat trailers piloted by nearsighted rookies.

5 CAMANCHE

Starting Point: *Jackson*
Distance: *54.2 miles*

Total Climb: *3,150 ft.*
Map: *Pages 14-15*

This loop will take you out and around the impressive Camanche Reservoir, while providing views of the expansive rolling hills from just about every possible direction. The western end of this loop travels through rolling open grass-covered hills; the eastern end tends to be a bit steeper and dotted with pines, madrones, and oaks. Springtime finds the green hills splashed with wildflowers. Summers can be both hot and crowded, with the boater traffic heading for this and nearby lakes. If you live in the Stockton or Sacramento areas you can easily start from Clements on Highway 88 or Ione on Highway 104.

From the Safeway lot in Jackson, go up Highway 49 to Martell and descend quickly down Highway 88 to Jackson Valley Road just past the road to Ione. Swing through sleepy Buena Vista and turn south about a mile later on Jackson Valley-Camanche Road. Here you will find small farms with well-kept summer gardens and horses grazing beside the road. Just beyond a gentle climb, turn west on Camanche

Stony Creek Road, looking north.

Parkway North and cross an arm of the reservoir a short distance later. The road is narrow and shoulderless, so be alert for boater traffic. Turn south on wide-open Highway 88, now on a shoulder, descend to the crossing of the Mokelumne River before turning east on Highway 12, which also has a good shoulder. Travel east on Camanche Parkway South, just past the Calaveras County line, where numerous beautiful views are found. Turn east at an unmarked 'T' intersection to continue on Camanche Parkway South, five miles past Highway 12. Cross an arm of the reservoir and begin delightfully playful Buena Vista Road, which climbs, drops, then climbs again. Turn east on Stony Creek Road where a little well sits in the center of the intersection. Stay with Stony Creek Road 10.5 miles through some marvelously expansive country with Digger pines and old stone fences before dropping into Jackson just north of where you began.

Railroad Flat Road, near Railroad Flat.

6 WEST POINT _____

Starting Point: *Jackson*
Distance: *52.5 miles*

Total Climb: *5,470 ft.*
Map: *Pages 14-15*

This route is a bit more challenging than the previous three but also more rewarding. There are some marvelous climbs and descents as well as gorgeous foothill scenery, lightly-traveled roads, and friendly small towns along the way. While measuring this route I happened to stumble onto a "Lumberjack Days" parade in West Point, which closed the highway for three hours. So I got a front row seat and watched the whole town and every horse within twenty miles parade by. That probably had a lot to do with the "good vibes" that carried over into Rail Road Flat too.

From the Safeway in Jackson take Highway 49 south .65 mile to Clinton Road and turn east. Stay on Clinton Road all the way to Pine Grove where a store can be found. Take Pine Grove-Volcano Road northeast and keep both hands on your brakes. Stop at Chaw-se Indian Grinding Rock State Park and see the nearly twelve-hundred mortar cups (Chaw-se) where Miwok Indians once lived and ground acorns for food. The local Indian community still uses the ritual dance house here; check with the ranger for schedules.

Continue on Pine Grove-Volcano Road. At the bottom of the second steep drop watch for the south turn onto Volcano-Pioneer Road. Now climb back up to Highway 88, then travel west (down hill) a very short distance before turning east on Red Corral Road (Hwy 26). After crossing the North Fork of the Mokelumne River (swimming hole), climb steadily through tall pines and red earth country, which levels out as you approach Main Street West Point. At the Historical Landmark (a plaque on a big stone), turn south to continue on Highway 26, which drops abruptly down to the Middle Fork of the Mokelumne. Turn southeast a half mile later to continue on Rail Road Flat Road through more drops and climbs before taking a break at one of the two stores in Rail Road Flat. Just beyond the second store, turn due west on Ridge Road, climb a bit more, then sail down to the Mokelumne Hill Threeway Road. Mokelumne Hill is a wonderful old town, so take the time to swing off Highway 49 by turning north on Main Street. To exit town, an east turn on Center Street takes you back to the highway. After your visit, another 6.4 easy miles on Highway 49 remain before returning to Jackson.

7 HWY 88—CARSON PASS _____

Starting Point: *Jackson*
Distance: *82.7 miles*

Total Climb: *9,120 ft.*
Map: *Pages 10-11, 30-31*

This is the first of four trans-Sierra passes presented in this guide. The others are Ebbetts Pass (Highway 4), Sonora Pass (Highway 108), and Tioga Pass (Highway 120). I show them not as day rides, though that is possible, but as connections to points east and for extended tours. Carson Pass is probably the most rideable of the four, due to the lower altitude, easier grades, and useable shoulder for all but twenty-eight miles. The upper portions, from Silver Lake to Markleeville, make superb day rides for those base camping in the Kirkwood or Sorensens Area. Carson Pass is also the only route that is kept open all year, not that I recommend trans-Sierra winter bicycle travel. Stores and roadhouses are fairly prevalent along Highway 88 so there is little concern about starvation and exposure. Now, motor homes, that's a different story.

Begin at the Safeway in Jackson and take Highway 88 east. The narrow shoulder extends for twenty-five miles to just below Cooks Station, where you will find a small store with restrooms. Regain the narrow shoulder below Mormon Emigrant Trail, where aspens and white fir combine for pleasant roadside scenery. Descend into the Silver Lake area and take a needed break at the store to rest and refuel. (See *Cyclists' Route Atlas, Sierra/North.* Route #24) Take it easy on Highway 88 between Silver Lake and Carson Pass; this road is shoulderless. But the scenery of Caples Lake backed by snowcapped peaks is breathtaking. If the weather is warm, take some time at the pass to reflect on the previous sixty-two miles before the well-deserved but much too short descent into unique Hope Valley, where high desert and high Sierra mix. The little resort of Sorensens will make a perfect place to regroup before continuing the long descent from the pass. Turn south at Woodfords on Highway 89/4 to Markleeville, climb a bit on a bike lane shoulder, and finish out in town, where a store and a couple of restaurants and hotels will take good care of you. If you can get a reservation, be sure to camp at Grover Hot Springs State Park just four miles west of Markleeville.

SAN ANDREAS

This quiet town was originally settled by Mexican miners in 1849 and has since lost much of the typical Gold Country flavor. Here you will find a full size store open seven days and some restaurants for after-cycling dining. Off-street parking is available east of Main Street. It makes a very good place to begin challenging day rides through the many miles of lightly-traveled back roads of western Calaveras County. These roads climb and play across open wind-swept ridges, roll and dance down warm forest-scented slopes, and rest, momentarily out of breath, before continuing on in search of adventures great and small.

8 JESUS MARIA

Starting Point: *San Andreas*
Distance: *37.9 miles*

Total Climb: *3,640 ft.*
Map: *Pages 24-25*

This beautiful route will take you up into one of the least visited and most enjoyable parts of the central Gold Country. The country you traverse changes from hilly open scrub to cool madrone, pine, and cedar filled valleys. The roads are old and rutted in places, but these routes, which traveled between mining camps of old, can take you back in time, if you let them.

From the grocery store and gas station in San Andreas, travel north, climbing gently on Highway 49 to Mokelumne Hill. Turn east onto Highway 26, then east again on Jesus Maria Road. The narrow road descends steeply, then winds along a cool creek, now on Grade Three pavement, before ascending through open, sometimes windy country. The settlement of Jesus Maria (pronounced Hey-soos) was destroyed by fire nearly 100 years ago and little remains other than a cemetery. The forest cover begins at mile 16.4 and provides welcome shade. Turn south on Rail Road Flat Road, now amongst tall pines, and descend easily to the hamlet of Mountain Ranch, the only settlement for miles around. A good store here makes a more than adequate refueling stop. Take your time on the fantastic but narrow descent via Mountain Ranch Road back to Highway 49.

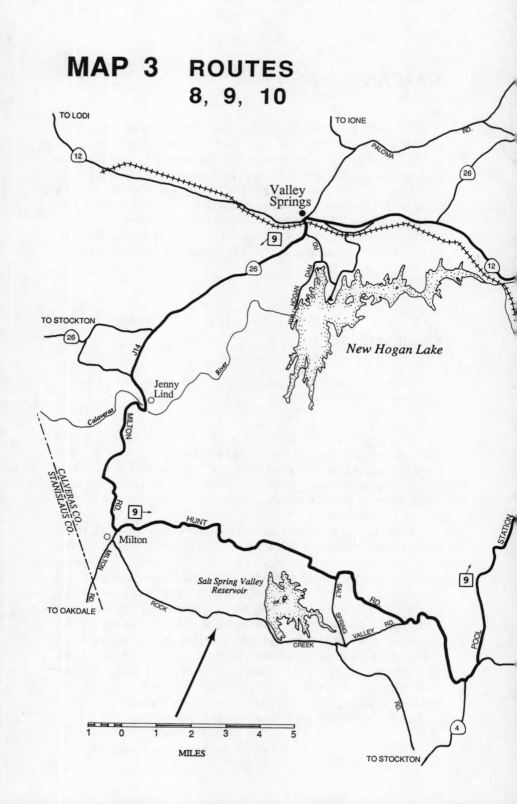

MAP 3　ROUTES
8, 9, 10

TO LODI

TO IONE

PALOMA RD.

12

26

Valley
Springs

9

26

HOGAN DAM RD.

12

TO STOCKTON

26

J14

River

New Hogan Lake

Jenny
Lind

Calaveras

MILTON

CALAVERAS CO.
STANISLAUS CO.

RD.

9

HUNT

STATION

Milton

9

Salt Spring Valley
Reservoir

SALT SPRING RD.

VALLEY RD.

MILTON RD.

ROCK

POOL

TO OAKDALE

CREEK

RD.

TO STOCKTON

4

MILES

1　0　1　2　3　4　5

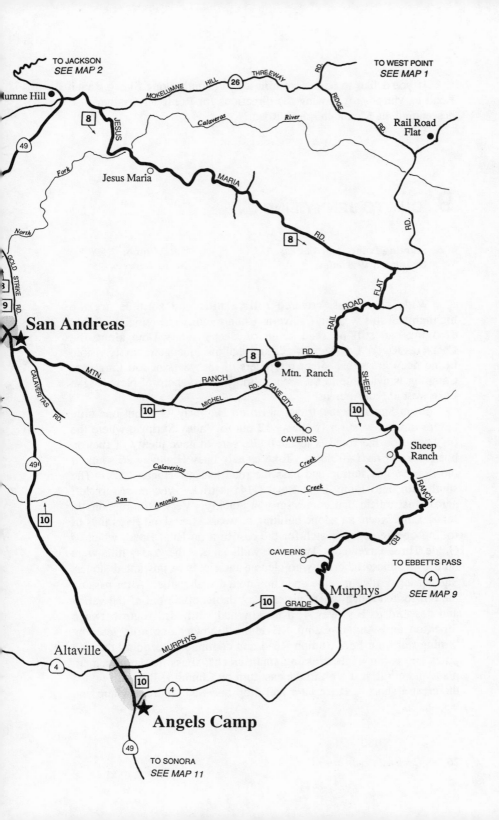

If you'd like to add more miles, head south along Sheep Ranch Road to Murphys following the directions for Route #10, rather than descending via Mountain Ranch Road.

9 OUT TO JENNY LIND

Starting Point: *San Andreas*
Distance: *49.8 miles*

Total Climb: *2,990 ft.*
Map: *Pages 24-25*

Wide open grass-covered rolling hills and solitude are the highlights of this western Calaveras County tour. The remains of gold dredging can still be seen south of sleepy Jenny Lind along the Calaveras River. Low stone walls and shallow aqueducts, barely visible in the deep grass, are silent reminders of the years of toil long ago. Camping is available in the area on the western shore of New Hogan Lake west of San Andreas.

From San Andreas, travel north on Highway 49 about one mile before turning west on Highway 12 out to Valley Springs, where the only store on the route is located. Be sure to have plenty of fuel on board for the next 40 miles. Take usually busy Highway 26 south at the Beacon gas station and pass the road to New Hogan Lake. The south turn onto Jenny Lind Road (J14) is tricky; you must turn left across fast traffic that comes on you quickly. Very little remains in Jenny Lind except an adobe building or two. After about five miles of rolling open country, watch for the east turn on Hunt Road, which is Grade Three Pavement. The stone walls among the grassy hills were built by Chinese laborers who cleared the fields of unwanted stones. Salt Spring Valley is wide open and dotted with cattle. After passing the red-roofed ranch where water is available, climb out of the valley and descend to Highway 4, a narrow and well-used route between Stockton and Angels Camp. Exit the highway one mile later by turning north on Pool Station Road and continue descending through pines and scrub while crossing small creeks. Pass the large cement plant and climb just a bit to the east turn on Church Hill Road. Reach the crest a short distance later and drop into San Andreas where you began.

Hunt Road, looking east.

ANGELS CAMP

Angels Camp was made famous by Mark Twain's "The Celebrated Jumping Frog of Calaveras County" and is probably the most well-know town along Highway 49. The town has many things for travelers to buy, eat, learn, and see along Main Street, including the "frog" that sits on a pedestal on the south end of town. Parking is limited, so be sure to arrive early on busy weekends. The Jumping Frog Contest is held every year in mid May and should be avoided if you plan to cycle in the area; it's a zoo. Inns are located in town, and campsites are at New Melones Reservoir to the south and at Calaveras Big Trees State Park on Highway 4. (See Route #11.) I don't really recommend this popular portion of Highway 49 to cyclists; it's heavily traveled and very narrow. If you avoid peak season and start early however, you should be all right. Other points of interest in the area are the town of Murphys and the limestone caverns near Vallecito.

Looking north from Mountain Ranch Road.

10 TO MURPHYS

Starting Point: *Angels Camp*
Distance: *43.9 miles*

Total Climb: *4,210 ft.*
Map: *Pages 24-25*

It's time to explore another challenging route through the eastern Gold Country, don't you think? I start this route in Angels Camp to get through with Highway 49 first thing in the morning, but you can start in San Andreas during non-peak times of the year. Murphys, with a fantastic tree-shaded main street, has some of the most pleasant and authentic ambience in the region. It also makes a great base camp.

Begin in Angels Camp and travel north on Highway 49 through Altaville. The shoulder disappears as you continue through mostly oak-shaded country before turning east on Mountain Ranch Road, just south of San Andreas. Ascend through Mountain Ranch, where the store is a welcome sight. Less than two miles later, turn southeast on Sheep Ranch Road and descend through open country and an occasional vineyard. Sheep Ranch is now a small collection of run-down houses, abandoned buildings, and an old fashioned gas pump with a glass top. Abandoned hardrock gold mines in the area were once operated by the rich and powerful Hearst family. Descend steeply, then climb steeply to the high point of the tour at 2,800 feet. A big drop followed by another steep climb in cool pine forest will take you past Mercer Cave and into Murphys. Wander through town, spend some time, and have some ice cream before continuing down the pleasant Murphys Grade to Altaville. Turn south on Highway 49 and return to Angels Camp.

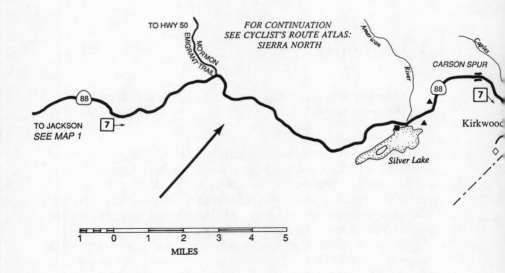

TO HWY 50

FOR CONTINUATION
SEE CYCLIST'S ROUTE ATLAS:
SIERRA NORTH

American River

Caples

MORMON EMIGRANT TRAIL

CARSON SPUR

88

7

88

7

TO JACKSON
SEE MAP 1

Kirkwood

Silver Lake

1   0   1   2   3   4   5
MILES

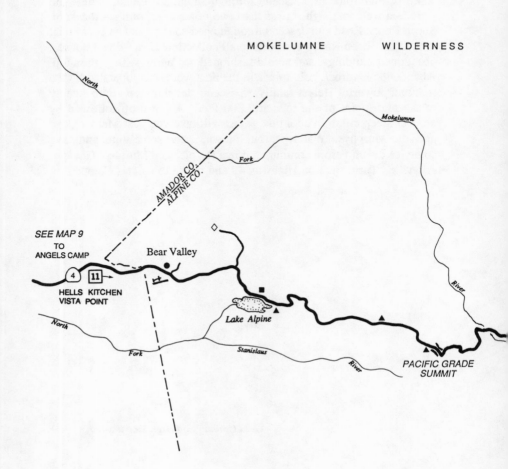

MOKELUMNE   WILDERNESS

North

Mokelumne

Fork

AMADOR CO.
ALPINE CO.

SEE MAP 9
TO
ANGELS CAMP

Bear Valley

4   11

HELLS   KITCHEN
VISTA   POINT

River

North

Lake Alpine

Fork

Stanislaus   River

PACIFIC GRADE
SUMMIT

MAP 4   ROUTES 7, END   11, END

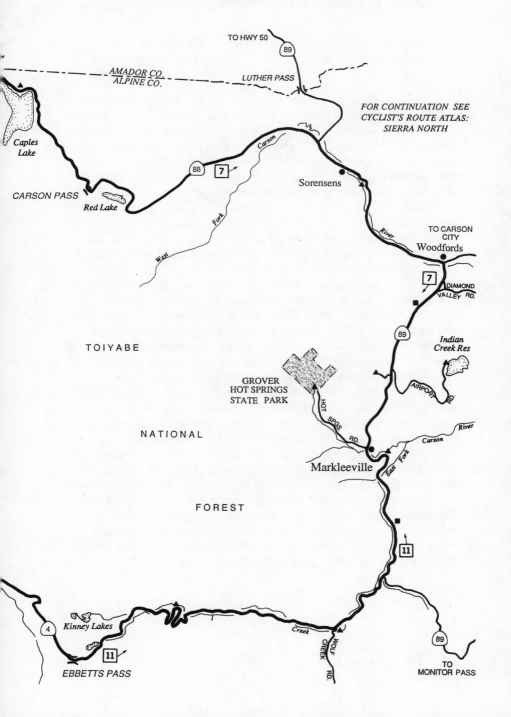

TO HWY 50

89

AMADOR CO.
ALPINE CO.

LUTHER PASS

FOR CONTINUATION SEE
CYCLIST'S ROUTE ATLAS:
SIERRA NORTH

Caples
Lake

Carson

88   7

Sorensens

CARSON PASS

Red Lake

River

TO CARSON
CITY
Woodfords

West   Fork

7

DIAMOND
VALLEY   RD.

89

Indian
Creek Res

TOIYABE

GROVER
HOT SPRINGS
STATE PARK

HOT   SPRGS   RD.

AIRPORT   RD.

NATIONAL

River

Carson

Markleeville

East   Fork

FOREST

11

4   Kinney Lakes

11

EBBETTS PASS

Creek

WOLF   CREEK   RD.

89

TO
MONITOR PASS

11 HWY 4—EBBETTS PASS

Starting Point: *Angels Camp*
Distance: *81.1 miles*

Total Climb: *9,300 ft.*
Map: *Pages 52-53, 30-31*

This trans-Sierra route takes you from Angels Camp past Calaveras Big Trees State Park, Lake Alpine, and over the 8,050 foot Pacific Grade and the 8,740 foot Ebbetts Pass before a white-knuckle descent into Markleeville. Generally speaking, the western portion of the route is not the best for riding because of the abundant, fast traffic. The eastern end of Highway 4, however, has some spectacular and challenging day rides, based from Markleeville or Lake Alpine.

From Angels Camp travel east on Highway 4. Ascend steadily, passing the road to Vallecito, then the road to Murphys. Small resort towns are at regular intervals all along the route, the largest among them is Arnold, twenty miles east of Angels Camp, with numerous restaurants and stores. Six miles beyond Arnold in Camp Connell the narrow-shouldered highway climbs steadily through pine forest. There is a Stanislaus National Forest campground to rest in and regroup, forty miles out of Angels Camp. Cross into Alpine County 4.5 miles later and pass a store a short distance beyond. The winter closure gates are just before the Lake Alpine Lodge, which serves great sandwiches on a panoramic porch overlooking the lake. The next 14.6 miles to Ebbetts Pass are truly beautiful High Sierra country, with dense forests, large meadows, clear cold streams, and expansive views of snow-capped peaks. The summit is yours when you cross the cattle-guard, so take a little breather in the shade. The road from the top was recently repaired, but rough spots and potholes still exist. Many of the turns are very tight and can have gravel on them, so take it easy. If you need water or a restroom, a campground 5.7 miles from the pass will provide both. Watch for another cattle-guard which signals a steep descent, then level out into a wide canyon with cedar and sage. Cross the East Fork of the Carson River and follow it as it slices a very colorful canyon most of the way to Markleeville, a delightful little burg surrounded by mountains on three sides. Camping is superb at Grover Hot Springs State Park, but be sure to get a reservation.

Highway 4, near Pacific Grade Summit.

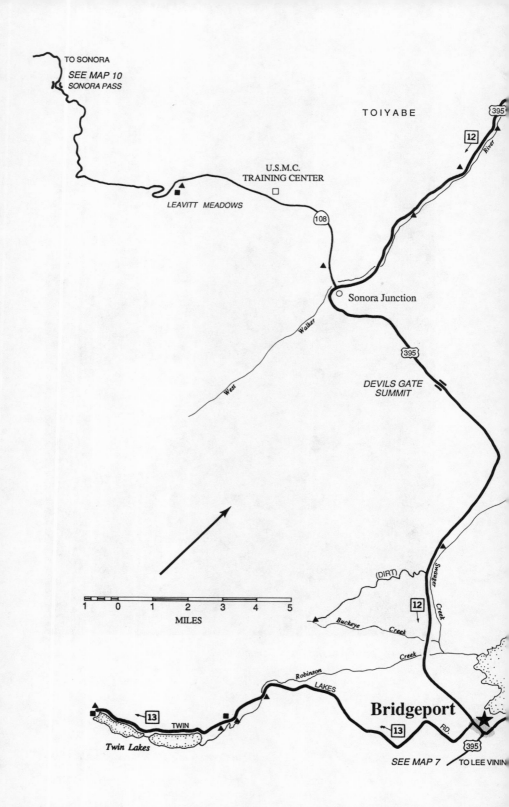

TO SONORA
SEE MAP 10
SONORA PASS

TOIYABE

395

12

River

U.S.M.C.
TRAINING CENTER

LEAVITT MEADOWS

108

Sonora Junction

Walker

395

*DEVILS GATE
SUMMIT*

West

12

(DIRT)

Swauger Creek

Buckeye Creek

Creek

1 0 1 2 3 4 5
MILES

Robinson

LAKES

Bridgeport

13

TWIN

13

RD.

Twin Lakes

395

SEE MAP 7   TO LEE VINING

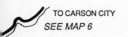

TO CARSON CITY
SEE MAP 6

MAP 5 ROUTES
12, SOUTH
13

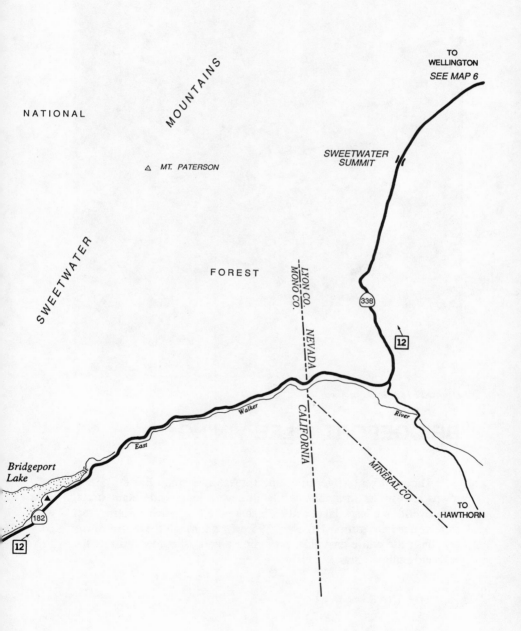

TO
WELLINGTON
SEE MAP 6

NATIONAL

MOUNTAINS

△ MT. PATERSON

SWEETWATER
SUMMIT

SWEETWATER

FOREST

LYON CO.
MONO CO.

NEVADA

338

12

Walker

River

East

CALIFORNIA

MINERAL CO.

Bridgeport
Lake

TO
HAWTHORN

182

12

Highway 182, looking north.

BRIDGEPORT & LEE VINING

Though twenty-five miles apart, these two small Eastern Sierra towns are similar in ambience. Both have a long, wide main street, both overlook a large lake, and both share the magnificent Sierra crest as a western backdrop. Highway 395 passes through these two towns and links the entire east side, providing a good shoulder most of the way and endless vistas.

Bridgeport is the larger of the two towns and has several motels, restaurants, and stores. Camping is good at nearby Twin Lakes (see Route #13) and at many sites along Highway 395. The enchanting Bodie State Historical Park is southeast of Bridgeport via Highway 270, the last few miles of which are gravel. This ghost town perched at 8,400 feet in the Bodie Hills, commands views over the surrounding desert landscape that evoke wonder and mystery. The remaining buildings have been preserved in what is termed "arrested decay". Ranger-led tours of the stamp mill and other buildings provide a richness missing from "tourist" towns. No services are available in Bodie.

Lee Vining has motels, restaurants, and other services. Serene Mono Lake to the east has been the source of controversy between the city of Los Angeles and environmental groups. Los Angeles has drawn off the fresh water inflow for many years, thereby greatly reducing the level of the lake and altering the surrounding eco-system. Recent wet years and court victories by environmentalists have slowed the decline. Mono Lake varies from tranquil to melancholy to exultant, but is always captivating. Highway 120 crosses Tioga Pass from Yosemite (see Route #22), descends just south of town, and offers a fabulous day ride to High Sierra splendor. The 9,950 foot pass is within two hours of steady riding from Lee Vining. More sage and pine country awaits via Highway 395 to the south past June Lake and Mammoth Mountain.

12 SWEETWATER

Starting Point: *Bridgeport*
Distance: *100.2 miles*

Total Climb: *4,590 ft.*
Map: *Pages 34-35, 38-39*

This gentle hundred mile loop is the most enjoyable ride I've done in many years. From Bridgeport through the first forty miles, my companion and I saw only half a dozen cars.

Head south from Bridgeport and turn north on Highway 182, which turns into 338 at the Nevada border. This early portion of the route is never steep and always interesting, with the Walker River below and snow-capped Mount Patterson above. On the pleasant ascent towards Sweetwater Summit, mirages shimmer and dance, obscuring

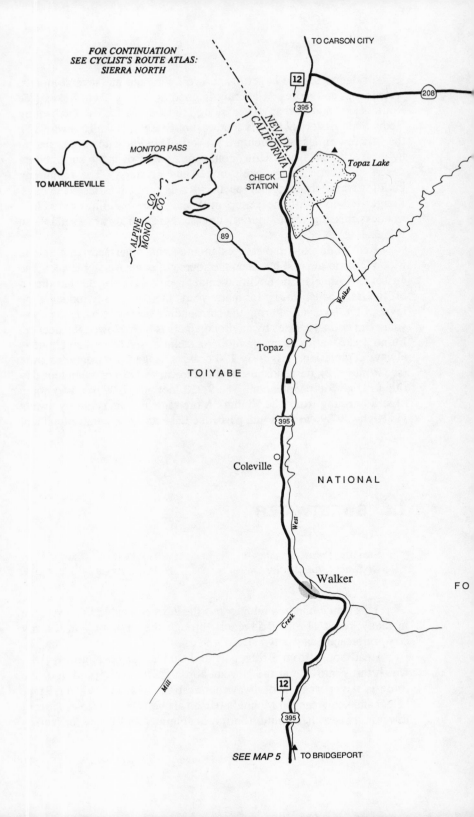

FOR CONTINUATION
SEE CYCLIST'S ROUTE ATLAS:
SIERRA NORTH

TO CARSON CITY

12

395

208

MONITOR PASS

NEVADA
CALIFORNIA

Topaz Lake

TO MARKLEEVILLE

CHECK
STATION

ALPINE CO.
MONO CO.

89

Walker

Topaz

TOIYABE

395

Coleville

NATIONAL

West

Walker

FO

Creek

Mill

12

395

SEE MAP 5 TO BRIDGEPORT

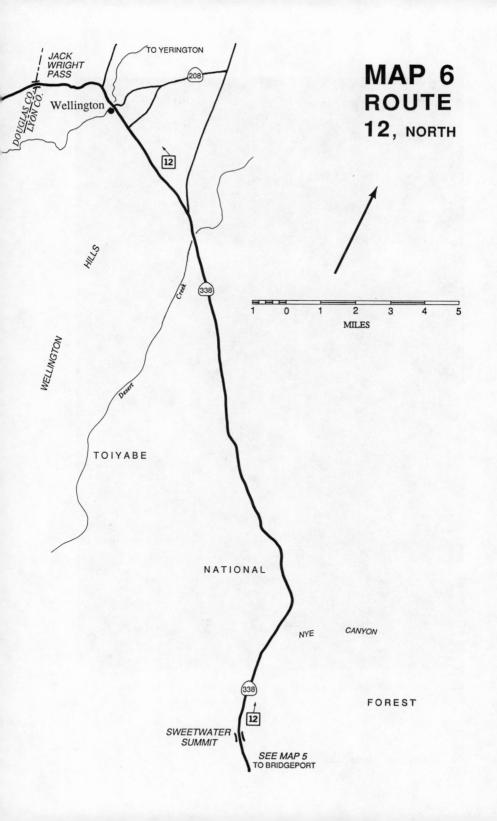

MAP 6
ROUTE
12, NORTH

JACK
WRIGHT
PASS

TO YERINGTON

208

Wellington

DOUGLAS CO.
LYON CO.

12

MILES

338

HILLS

Creek

WELLINGTON

Desert

TOIYABE

NATIONAL

NYE   CANYON

338

12

FOREST

SWEETWATER
SUMMIT

SEE MAP 5
TO BRIDGEPORT

Looking west over Bridgeport Lake.

the pavement and giving the false sense of road and sky being one. Miles of colorful canyon with sage and pinyon pine are traversed before you arrive in Wellington at the south end of a wide agricultural valley. The small store there is closed Sundays, but services are available twelve miles further near Topaz Lake.

Ascend to Jack Wright Pass and continue eastward before turning south on Highway 395. Cross into California at the agricultural check station along shoulderless highway while passing to the west of Topaz Lake. The long ascent via Highway 395 beyond Walker along the West Fork of the Walker River is narrow and well-traveled, so be alert for other traffic. Campgrounds along the highway can provide water and restrooms. Pass Sonora Junction, the eastern end of Highway 108 (see Route #18) where a Cal-trans maintenance station is a lonely outpost. Devils Gate Summit is a welcome sight and signals the end of the climb and the beginning of eleven miles of descent, past a sheep ranch and into the lush green valley surrounding Bridgeport where you began. A campground on Buckeye Creek is thirteen miles west of town via dirt road and has good sites and a primitive hot spring. Enjoy.

13 TWIN LAKES

Starting Point: *Bridgeport*	**Total Climb:** *680 ft.*
Distance: *27.2 miles*	**Map:** *34-35*

If some among you aren't about to pedal one hundred miles, have no fear. This easy route to Twin Lakes should provide a worthy alternate with nothing lost in terms of scenery and beauty. As you ride into this wide flat canyon, numerous peaks of over 12,000 feet loom proudly above you.

From the west end of Bridgeport, take Twin Lakes Road south. Pass the Hospital, and traverse green meadows where cattle graze. Ascend gradually, never steeper than 2.6%, while passing numerous campgrounds and a store at mile 10.3. Another store at the upper end of Upper Twin Lake is a pleasant end point where boat rentals, fishing, swimming, and sunning are favorites. Any one of the many

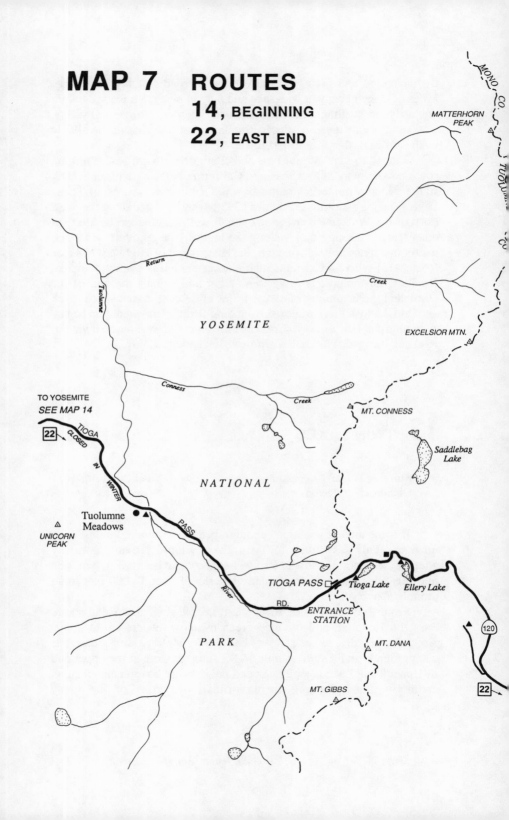

MAP 7 **ROUTES**
14, BEGINNING
22, EAST END

MONO CO.

MATTERHORN
PEAK

TUOLUMNE CO.

Return

Creek

Tuolumne

YOSEMITE

EXCELSIOR MTN.

Conness

Creek

TO YOSEMITE
SEE MAP 14

MT. CONNESS

22 TIOGA

CLOSED IN WINTER

Saddlebag
Lake

NATIONAL

Tuolumne
Meadows

UNICORN
PEAK

PASS

TIOGA PASS □ Tioga Lake Ellery Lake

River

RD.

ENTRANCE
STATION

120

PARK

MT. DANA

22

MT. GIBBS

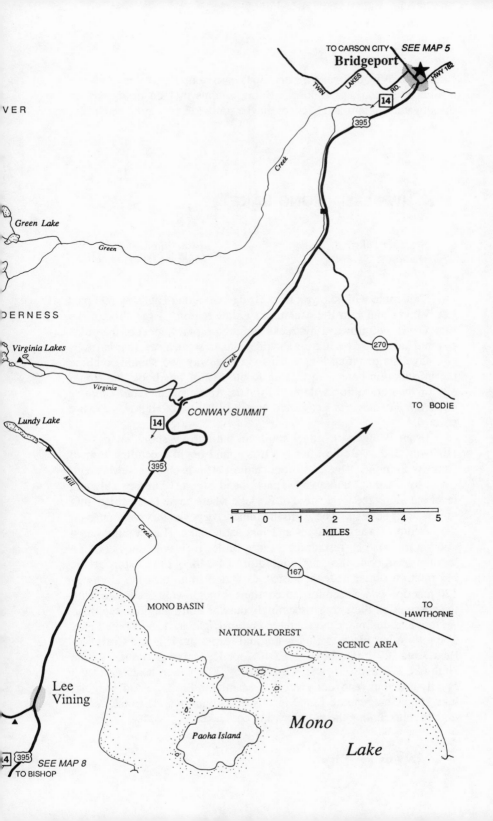

campgrounds would make a marvellous base camp from which to begin a number of cycling sojourns. Some options include riding east to Sweetwater Summit and back, or maybe south to Lee Vining and back.

14 HWY 395—MONO LAKE _____

Starting Point: *Bridgeport*　　　　**Total Climb:** *4,160 ft.*
Distance: *54.4 miles*　　　　　　　**Map:** *Pages 42-43, 46-47*

　　　This route will take you from Bridgeport along Highway 395 past Lee Vining and into the Mammoth Lakes region. Even though the highway is well traveled by trucks and motorhomes, most of the miles covered have at least a narrow shoulder and, in some areas, four lanes.
　　　Cyclists planning longer trips via Highway 395 should combine the information here with that on Route #12 of this book and Route #26 of the companion volume, *Cyclists' Route Atlas: Gold Country and High Sierra/North*. Together, nearly 120 miles of Highway 395 are covered.
　　　From Bridgeport, travel south on the narrow shoulder, passing Highway 270 to Bodie after 6.9 miles, and begin ascending toward Conway Summit. The 8,140 foot summit affords endless views south over Mono Lake, Mammoth Mountain, and beyond. Drop quickly and level out along the west shore of the lake where some fascinating "tufa towers" can be seen. These are the mineral deposits that were once on the bottom of a much larger and less saline lake. Lee Vining has a good store, motels, restaurants, and a trailer park with showers. To learn more about the past and future of Mono Lake, stop at the information center near the store. Continue south past the Highway 120 junction into Yosemite and continue through wide open sage, with the everpresent Sierra crest seemingly only an arm's length to the west. A store and deli mark the southern end of Highway 158 to June Lake. The only other place to find water and restrooms is at the Crestview Rest Area 3.7 miles beyond 8,040 foot Deadman Summit. Leave Highway 395 and turn west on Highway 203, which leads up to the rapidly growing year-round resort of Mammoth Lakes. Food, lodging, bike shops, etc. can be found in this year-round resort, so take some time to relax among the tall pines and cool lakes.

Looking south over Mono Lake from Conway Summit.

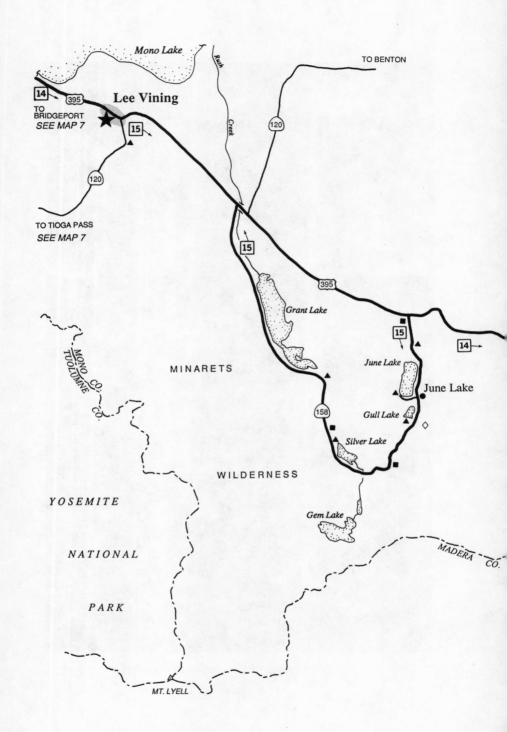

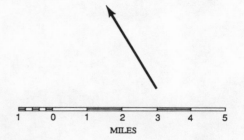

MAP 8 ROUTES
14, SOUTH END
15, 16

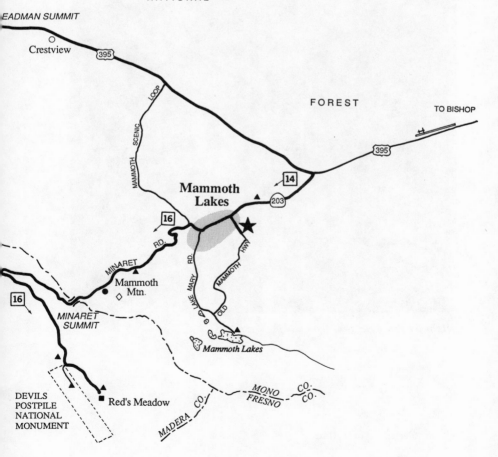

INYO

1 0 1 2 3 4 5
MILES

NATIONAL

EADMAN SUMMIT

Crestview

○

395

LOOP

FOREST

TO BISHOP

MAMMOTH SCENIC

395

14

Mammoth
Lakes

203

16

★

RD.

16

MINARET

MINARET
SUMMIT

Mammoth
Mtn.

◇

●

LAKE MARY RD.

OLD MAMMOTH HWY.

Mammoth Lakes

DEVILS
POSTPILE
NATIONAL
MONUMENT

Red's Meadow

■

MADERA CO.

MONO CO.
FRESNO CO.

Highway 158, near June Lake looking West.

15 JUNE LAKE

Starting Point: *Lee Vining*
Distance: *31.7 miles*

Total Climb: *1,140 ft.*
Map: *Pages 46-47*

This is one of the finest, most enjoyable loops in the Sierra. The imposing peaks sparkling lakes rimmed with cool aspen groves, and wide open sage, create a truly beautiful environment. This loop is well within the reach of almost any cyclist with a sense of adventure. If riding on Highway 395 seems to be too much, try starting from the little store at the southern Highway 158/ Highway 395 junction and ride as far around the lake as you like.

From Lee Vining travel south along highway 395 and ascend gradually through wide open sage. The striking Mono Craters can be seen to the east and are evidence of past volcanic activity throughout the region. Turn southwest on Highway 158 and come face to face with the massive Sierra crest. Stores and restaurants can be found in June Lake as well as hotels and campgrounds. Two other lakes, Silver Lake and Grant Lake, are toured before returning to open sage country and Highway 395. Turn north there and end in Lee Vining where you began.

16 RED'S MEADOW

Starting Point: *Mammoth Lakes*
Distance: *30.6 miles*

Total Climb: *1,530 ft.*
Map: *Pages 46-47*

This is a great training ride for Mammoth Lakes locals and a challenging day ride over the 9,180 foot Mineret Summit to Devils Postpile National Monument. Red's Meadow is a popular pack station and trailhead into the John Muir Wilderness. Devils Postpile National Monument is a truly unique place where columns of basalt rock, looking like huge honeycomb, stand exposed, cut and polished by glacial activity centuries ago.

From the Safeway lot in Mammoth Lakes, travel north on Old

Mammoth Highway to Highway 203 and turn west. A bike lane shoulder can be followed to Minaret Road which veers north where the sign says "To Devils Postpile and Red's Meadow". Climb steadily through a stately fir and pine forest before easing off at the Mammoth Mountain Ski Resort. The automobile access from here to Devils Postpile is limited, which greatly reduces the traffic and parking problems found below. After crossing the summit, you descend to Agnew Meadows on a very narrow road, so be alert for other traffic. Notice too, the evidence of avalanche as you descend. Several campgrounds are located in this wonderful valley, at the end of which is the bustling horse and mule pack station at Red's Meadow. A store and cafe are here, as well as cabins for rent by the day or by the week. The return trip is easy; well, at least the road is easy to follow and not get lost. The climb is a bit tough, but the descent back to Mammoth Lakes is wonderful.

Other paved roads in the area worth exploring are Mammoth Scenic Loop and Lake Mary Road. Stop in at the bike shop south of the starting point for any assistance.

SONORA & COLUMBIA

Though not the largest town in the Mother Lode, Sonora is certainly one of the most spirited. Located at Highways 49 and 108, Main Street is often crowded with tourists headed for or returning from the mountains. The newly completed Highway 108 Sonora bypass should bring welcome relief from the weekend crush. The downtown area has many beautiful buildings, including the Episcopal Church and the I.O.O.F. (Odd Fellows) Hall. Of course, there is the ever-present ice cream soda fountain to feed the sweet tooth. Narrow bustling streets lined by raised sidewalks and awnings recall a bygone day. I don't think the original Forty-niners envisioned motorhomes pulling ski boats through their towns. The Sonora routes all start from the Safeway lot on Highway 108 just south of the Downtown area . The town also has a good bike shop.

Columbia State Historic Park five miles north of Sonora, is a wonderfully restored town. The shady pedestrian-only streets are great

Meadow below Minaret Summit.

MAP 9 ROUTES 11, BEGINNING
17,
18, BEGINNING

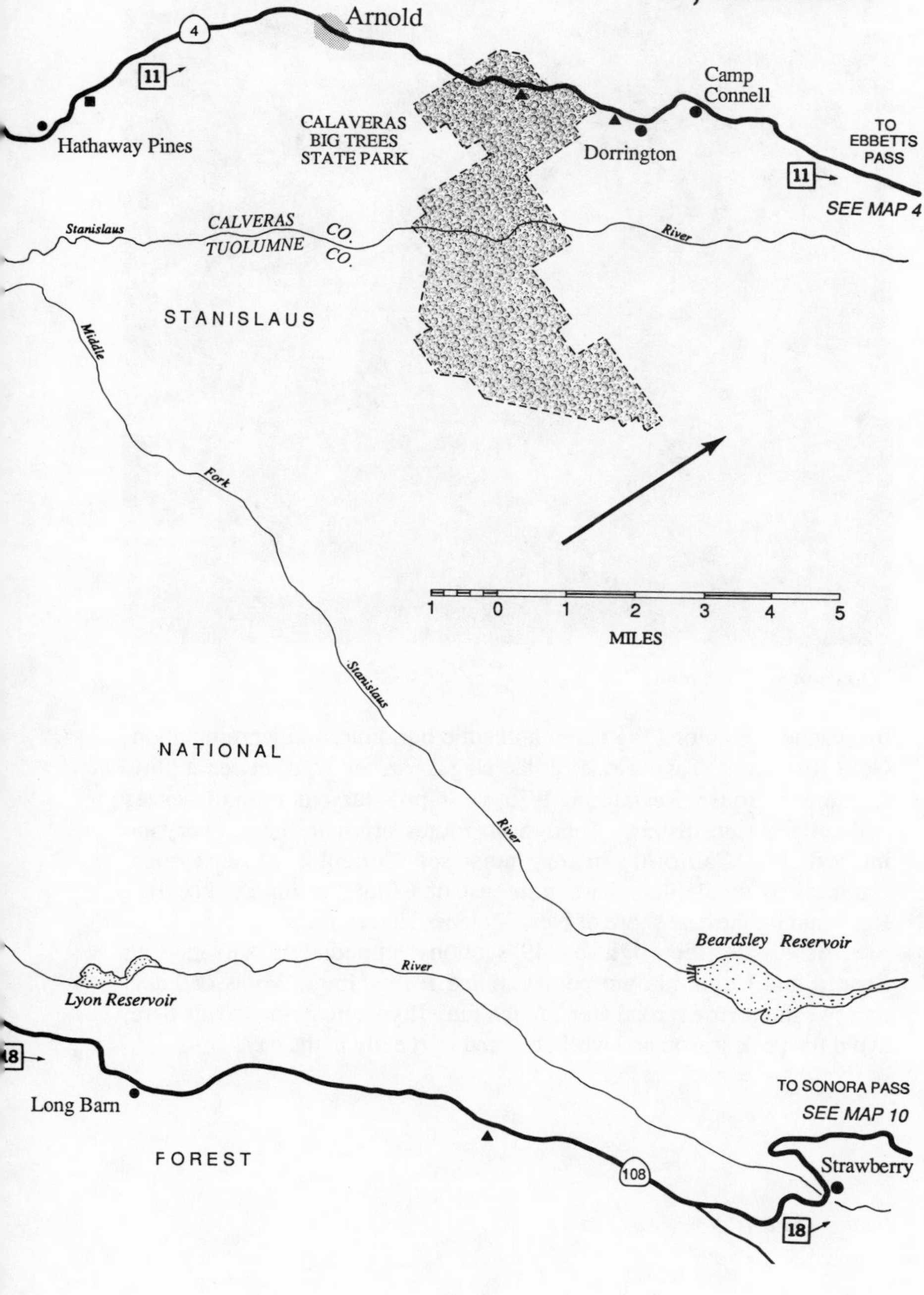

4

11

Arnold

Hathaway Pines

CALAVERAS
BIG TREES
STATE PARK

Camp
Connell

Dorrington

TO
EBBETTS
PASS

11

SEE MAP 4

Stanislaus   CALVERAS   CO.   *River*
                   TUOLUMNE   CO.

STANISLAUS

Middle

Fork

Stanislaus

NATIONAL

River

```
1   0   1   2   3   4   5
          MILES
```

Beardsley Reservoir

River

Lyon Reservoir

18

TO SONORA PASS
SEE MAP 10

Long Barn

Strawberry

FOREST

108

18

"Downtown" Columbia.

for wandering among the many authentic buildings and learning about Gold Rush life. Take a ride on the stage, pan for gold, or see a play. Columbia House Restaurant is a very popular eatery and serves authentic period dishes. Though no routes originate here, everyone interested in California history must see Columbia at least once. Camping is available a half mile east of Columbia on Yankee Hill Road and on the east shore of New Melones Reservoir.

As a rule, the Highway 49 sections immediately surrounding Sonora and Columbia are poorly suited for cycling. Miles of busy, narrow, shoulderless road aren't much fun. If you are going to ride here, avoid the peak season and weekends and start early in the day.

17 COLUMBIA

Starting Point: *Sonora*
Distance: *36.0*

Total Climb: *2,600 ft.*
Map: *Pages 52-53*

This short route travels through the country well known to Mark Twain. I'm not sure if Mark and his buddies ever rode their bikes through these hills, but the challenge is certainly open to you. Here too, the traffic on this section of Highway 49 is a negative factor for cycling. On the other hand, Parrots Ferry Road is much less traveled since the Stanislaus River was inundated by New Melones and the high bridge was built. This landscape is characterized by open grass- and scrub-covered hills, oaks and pines, and numerous quartz outcroppings.

Begin at the Safeway lot, travel north through downtown Sonora, and follow Highway 49 out of town. Pass the Columbia turn off (E18) after three miles. Descend westward, still on Highway 49, through cool, tree-shaded areas. Continue into open areas with views to the south and west. Pass the roads to the once-famous sites of Shaws Flat and Tuttletown before crossing the western high bridge over the New Melones Reservoir. Having spent many wonderful summer weekends rafting on the now inundated Stanislaus River, I must admit that I do not find this body of water a pleasant sight.

Climb out past the once gold-rich area of Carson Hill. Turn east on Highway 4 at the southern outskirts of Angels Camp and climb over some easy rolling hills before leaving the highway on Angels Road and turning into Vallecito, a town that consists of well-kept houses, a post office, and a few boarded up stone buildings, but no store. Turn south on narrow Parrots Ferry Road and pass the road to Moaning Cave a half mile later. This large interesting limestone cavern was said to have "moaned" until a staircase was built inside it in the early twenties and spoiled the acoustics. After crossing the eastern high bridge over New Melones, climb about 900 feet and cruise into Columbia. There is much to see and do here, so be sure to take a break and tour the town. Leave Columbia by traveling south to join with busy Highway 49 and continue to Sonora.

One shorter alternative to this route is to ride from Sonora to Columbia and back. But I bet you already thought of that.

18 HWY 108—SONORA PASS

Starting Point: *Sonora*
Distance: *79.8 miles*

Total Climb: *9,990 ft.*
Map: *Pages 52-53, 58-59*

So, you're lookin' for a fun little day ride. Not too long, but plenty of nice views, right? Well, this ISN'T it! This, the third trans-Sierra route presented so far, is probably the toughest of the bunch. Beyond Kennedy Meadows, the road climbs steeply at 9.4% for over six miles and has a few pitches over 15%. I don't mean to tell you your business, but cycling over this is hard work. The east side descent is really fun, too. The steepest drop in the book is found here: almost 19%, or one thousand feet per mile. How are your brakes?

From Sonora, get onto Highway 108 and ride east out of town. Stores and services are fairly plentiful along the route, usually about ten miles apart or less. As you ascend, tree cover changes from the oaks and pines of the warmer areas below to the cedars and sugar pines with their cool wonderful aroma. A shoulder comes and goes and ends about 7.5 miles below Strawberry. Campgrounds become common above 6,000 feet and are good sources of water. Over 800 feet are lost on the descent to Dardanelle where a store, a restaurant, and lodge are open seven days a week. Here the narrow highway is well guarded by huge majestic pines, which come right to the pavement edge. The last west-side store is a mile off the highway at Kennedy Meadows. This popular pack station, trail head, and campground make a nice place to rest up and re-group for the morning assault on the pass. 3,400 feet must be ascended in the next nine miles. Are you sure you still want to do this? Ride through granite outcroppings and beside green meadows with little snow-fed creeks before the top is reached, a magnificent sight. The views west and east stretch out into the haze for hundreds of miles. It will probably be cool up there, so bundle up for the chilly descent ahead.

A basic cyclist's rule says, "Never trust a highway sign," and the next two signs are no exception. The first sign says "15% drop" where it never exceeds 12% and the second says "10% 1 mile" but it doesn't make that either. The big lie comes on the drop just above Leavitt Meadows. Is there a sign warning of the 18% pitch to come? NO! Leavitt Meadows has a small store and cabins for rent at very reasonable rates. A Marine Corps Mountain Warfare Training Center is just ahead where recruits play hide-and-go-seek in the rocks. One more

Highway 108, near Kennedy Meadows.

MAP 10 ROUTE
18, EAST END

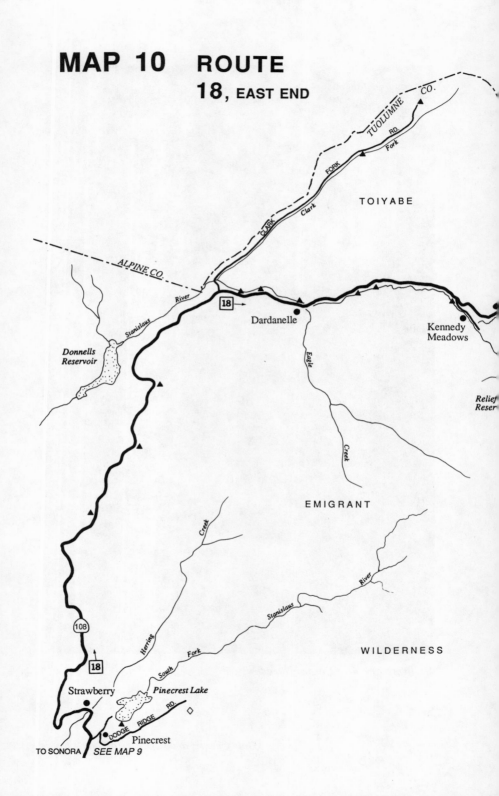

TUOLUMNE CO.

CLARK FORK RD.

Fork

TOIYABE

ALPINE CO.

River

CLARK FORK

Clark

18

Dardanelle

Stanislaus

Eagle

Kennedy
Meadows

Donnells
Reservoir

Relief
Reser

Creek

EMIGRANT

Creek

River

Stanislaus

108

18

South Fork

Herring

WILDERNESS

Strawberry

Pinecrest Lake

DODGE RIDGE RD.

Pinecrest

TO SONORA   SEE MAP 9

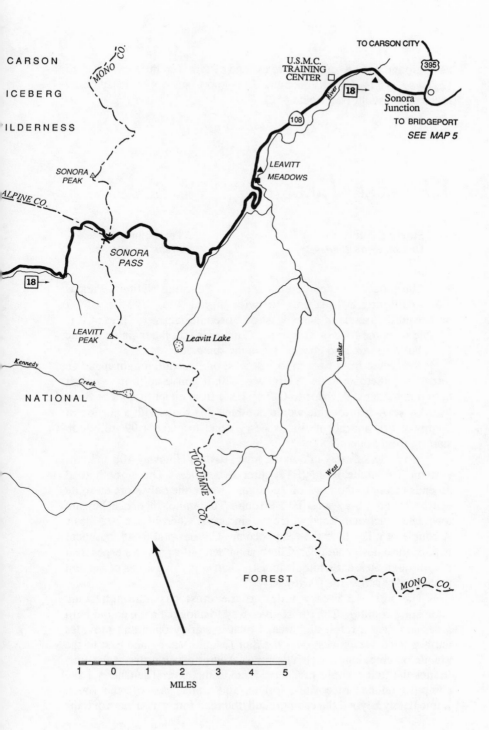

CARSON

ICEBERG

ILDERNESS

MONO CO.

SONORA
PEAK

ALPINE CO.

SONORA
PASS

18

LEAVITT
PEAK

Leavitt Lake

Kennedy

Creek

NATIONAL

TUOLUMNE CO.

TO CARSON CITY

395

U.S.M.C.
TRAINING
CENTER

River

18

Sonora
Junction

108

TO BRIDGEPORT
SEE MAP 5

LEAVITT
MEADOWS

Walker

West

FOREST

MONO CO.

1   0   1   2   3   4   5
MILES

campground can be found before the end of this "fun little day ride" on Highway 395 at Sonora Junction. Bridgeport is about seventeen easy miles to the south (see Route #12).

19 CHERRY LAKE

Starting Point: *Sonora*
Distance: *64.2 miles*

Total Climb: *7,760 ft.*
Map: *Pages 62-63*

The lonely forested country west of Yosemite National Park is worth exploring at least once or twice in your life. The fire of '87 destroyed thousands of acres west of Yosemite, but very little of it is visable from the road on this route. Timber is still the main economic base, but cattle are also grazed here in the summer.

This route from Sonora to just west of Yosemite might make an interesting alternate route to Highway 120, if you're up to it. Another option is to take a day ride to Cherry Lake from either Sonora or Buck Meadows. A real toughie would combine this route with a portion of Highway 120 and all of Wards Ferry Road to make a 99 mile loop starting from Sonora.

From the Safeway in Sonora, travel east on Highway 108 and turn east on Tuolumne Road (E17) after two miles. The smooth road ascends nicely to the town of Tuolumne, where the only store en-route can be found. Stay with E17 through Tuolumne, then just beyond town take Buchanan Road where the sign says "Cherry Lake 30 Miles". A couple of miles later the road becomes Cottonwood Road, but there is no sign to designate this. Climb about ten miles, never steeper than 8%, through pleasant white fir forest. Then enjoy five miles of descent to the bridge across the Clavey River.

The next 12.5 easy miles to the crest pass through some interesting country. The forest gives way to a logged area, an old burn area, and then a reforested area, which is starkly open and provides unobstructed views west over the San Joaquin Valley and east to the granite outcroppings above Yosemite. A large aspen grove at the crest frames the first glimpse of Cherry Lake to the east. The Cherry Lake campground has nice sites, toilets, and water, just off the route. Immediately beyond the campground, the road forks. You can continue

Cherry Lake.

on by heading straight south or detouring .25 mile to the lake. Oh, what the heck, you've come this far, might as well go and stick your feet in the water. There is a boat ramp there and a Ranger Station with a phone just above the lake.

Continuing on, cross the cattle-guard and prepare for 8.2 miles of marvellous descent into "The Grand Canyon of the Tuolumne". The climb out to the west end of Mather Road is not so marvellous but doesn't last long. Highway 120 is only 5.3 miles away (6 miles according to the sign) and all downhill!

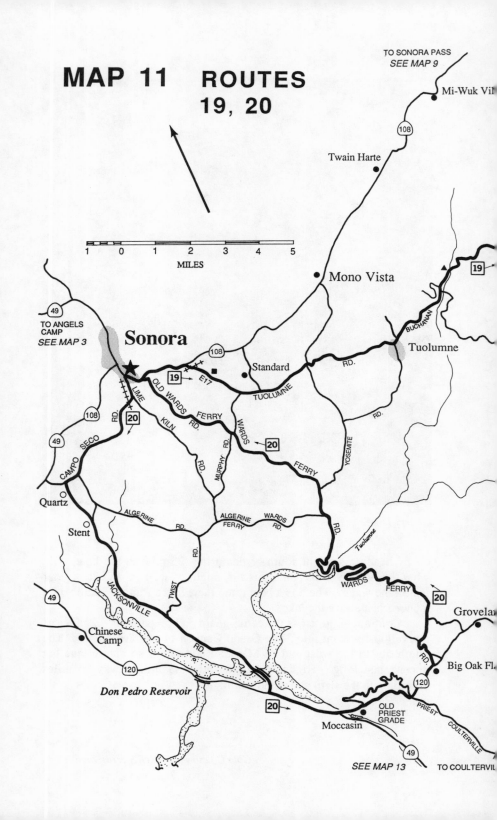

Wards Ferry Road, beyond Big Oak Flat.

20 WARDS FERRY _____

Starting Point: *Sonora* **Total Climb:** *4,410 ft.*
Distance: *39.3 miles* **Map:** *Pages 62-63*

Warning! This route should not to be attempted by the weak of
knee or faint of heart. This is the most painful hill in the Sierras. If,
for some reason, you find yourself riding this little gem and your legs
turn to jello at Moccasin, don't blame me. You can wimp out by
taking Highway 120 up to Big Oak Flat instead. Pheew! But wait!
There is still the oppressively hot climb on Wards Ferry to contend
with. Oh damn!

This is the final warning.

Begin in Sonora from (you guessed it) the Safeway and take Lime
Kiln Road south about .7 mile, cross the new highway, and turn
southwest on Campo Seco Road. Cross a set of railroad tracks, then
turn south on Jacksonville Road. The road passes through the sites of
Quartz and Stent. Both were destroyed by fire around the turn of the
century, and no original buildings remain, only modern homes.

Jacksonville Road ends after crossing Moccasin Reservoir at
Highway 120/49. Take the wide-shouldered highway south past the
Highway 49 exit. Pass above the Moccasin fish hatchery, turn east on
Old Priest Grade, and say your prayers. That funny odor is from molten
brakes on the cars that survive this two mile short-cut down from
Priest. (I always knew those old priests were a fun loving lot.)

Assuming you get to the top at Highway 120, the hot open scrub
country turns to life-saving shady pine cover. A cafe a mile further east
is a good bet for a rest stop. At .5 mile beyond the cafe, take Wards
Ferry Road north. Crest out, then drop quickly on smooth pavement to
the fork where you continue north. The pavement turns abruptly to
Grade Three a half mile further at another fork, where you turn north
(right). Take it very easy here; the narrow, steep, bumpy road has no
guard-rail. The wide modern bridge, also a rafters' take-out point, seems
out of place as you cross the Tuolumne River. Climb out immediately
and be sure to have plenty of water for the next 3.5 miles of exposed
south-facing hillside. Crest out and continue on Wards Ferry Road,
passing the Algerine Wards Ferry Road intersection. Rolling grass-
covered hills, red earth and Digger Pines, and small farms dot the area as
you swing west on Old Wards Ferry Road at a pond. Follow this road
back out to Highway 108 just above Sonora and the Safeway where you
began. "Hey, that wasn't as bad as you said. I'm gonna do it again."

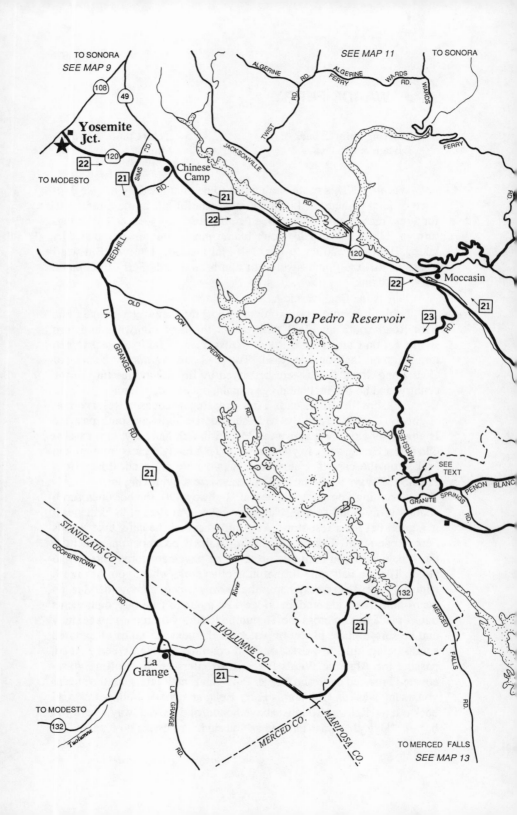

MAP 12   ROUTES 21,
22, BEGINNING
23

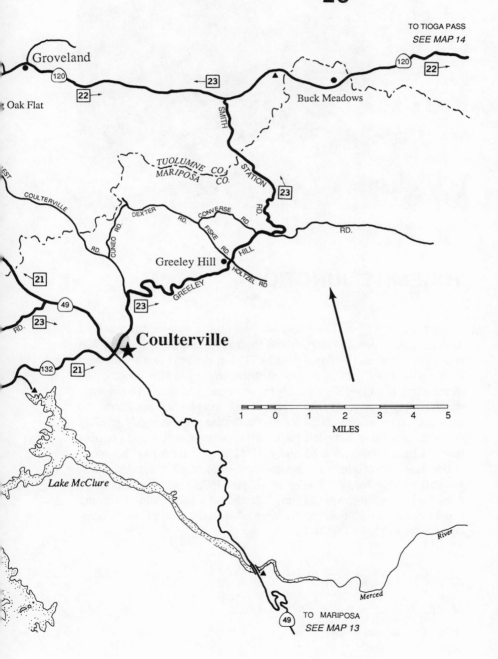

TO TIOGA PASS
SEE MAP 14

Groveland

120

23

120

22

22

Oak Flat

Buck Meadows

TUOLUMNE CO.
MARIPOSA   CO.

SMITH STATION RD.

23

COULTERVILLE

DEXTER   RD.   CONVERSE   RD.

RD.

FISKE   RD.

RD.

CUNEO   RD.

Greeley Hill

HILL

HOLTZEL RD.

GREELEY

21

49

23

23

RD.

132

21

★ **Coulterville**

1   0   1   2   3   4   5
MILES

Lake McClure

River

Merced

49

TO MARIPOSA
SEE MAP 13

Looking south from La Grange Road.

YOSEMITE JUNCTION

This starting point at Yosemite Junction is nothing more than a roadside gas station and store where Highway 120 meets Highway 108 about ten miles southwest of Sonora. I start the next two routes here because of easy access for those traveling from the west. The surrounding country differs greatly between east and west. To the west, gentle rolling grasslands with scattered oak and pine are the norm. To the east, steep brushy hillsides and tall pines are found. Ancient volcanic lava flows have left butte-like tablelands with shear crumbly faces. Chinese labor cleared many fields of their numerous boulders, also volcanic in origin, and painstakingly built miles of fences, which are still visable today. Rustic or elegant lodgings are available in numerous towns in the area from Columbia to Coulterville. Camping is plentiful too on all three of the large lakes in the area: New Melones, Don Pedro, and Lake McClure.

21 AROUND DON PEDRO

Starting Point: *Yosemite Jct.*
Distance: *64.2 miles*

Total Climb: *3,780 ft.*
Map: *Pages 66-67*

This is a very pleasant day ride, fairly gentle, and always interesting in the variety of country and history traversed. From Yosemite Junction follow Highway 120 east to Sims Road and turn south. Cross a small creek and continue south, now on Redhill Road. Turn south again on La Grange Road (J59) at the beautiful old stone corral under a shady oak tree. Lovely, rolling, grassy hills are the format for the journey down to Highway 132 and La Grange. This quiet town has a legacy of heavy dredge mining on the Tuolumne River north of town. Famous author Bret Harte was a school teacher in La Grange for a short period of time as well. A classy old country store here is not to be missed. More rolling hills are waiting to the east on narrow but lightly-traveled Highway 132 as you hop between three counties; Stanislaus, Tuolumne, and Mariposa. An exhilarating but short plunge past Lake McClure is followed by a good climb out to one of my favorite towns, Coulterville. If you can, spend some time here, or plan to come back for some home cookin' at Maxwell Station restaurant.

The next few miles on Highway 49 are usually lonely and always pleasant as you roll along through Digger Pine and chaparral. Crest out at the Tuolumne County line and watch for a tight hair-pin turn half way down this exhilarating descent. Join Highway 120 at Moccasin Reservoir and ride the wide shoulder to Chinese Camp. A small store on the highway and many unique buildings off the highway mark this picturesque old town. Continue on a narrow shoulder, passing Sims Road and the lumber mill, ending at the store at Yosemite Junction.

22 HWY 120—TIOGA PASS

Starting Point: *Yosemite Jct.*　　**Total Climb:** *12,700 ft.*
Distance: *111.5 miles*　　**Map:** *Pages 66-67, 80-81, 42-43*

The fourth and final trans-Sierra route, Tioga Pass, at 9,941 feet is the loftiest piece of pavement in the state. Most of Highway 120 is less than ideal for cycling. In a addition to Yosemite's millions of yearly visitors, the entire length of highway within the park is shoulderless. Cyclists usually have a tough time here. That's not to say the country isn't effusively beautiful, challenging, and grand; it is. Riding through Yosemite will continue to be the ambition of many

Looking east over Tenaya Lake.

cyclists, so here you go. Actually, riding east to west isn't so bad. You can usually keep up with the existing traffic. Campgrounds usually fill up so be sure to get reservations ahead of time. For more on Yosemite Park see Routes #25 through #28.

Begin at Yosemite Junction and head east on Highway 120, which soon joins with Highway 49 near Chinese Camp. These hills are very warm in summer months so try to begin in the early morning. Climb steadily from Moccasin, where a store can be found below the highway, and congratulate yourself for having the intelligence to not attempt the Old Priest Grade shortcut (see Route #20). Groveland is the largest of the small towns west of Yosemite and has a pleasant park in which to rest. Some of the worst destruction from the '87 fire happened in the area between Groveland and Yosemite. New highway beyond Groveland is pleasantly graded with wide shoulder that ends in Buck Meadows, the last services before Yosemite. This little resort area was the site of some truly heroic efforts by the firefighters. Four men lost their lives, here but almost all the homes and buildings were saved. The damage will surely heal with time but it is a stark reminder of the power of nature. Plenty of uphill remains before rolling through the Big Oak Flat entrance station and into Yosemite National Park. Cyclists pay only 50¢ to enter (cars pay $3.00). Restrooms, park information, and a coke machine are available here too. The remaining 67.3 miles of Highway 120 have no shoulder, so be extra careful and avoid weekend travel if possible. After the second descent, turn north at Crane Flat, which has a store open from 9 to 6 every day. You will pass many informative roadside exhibits on the geology, the history, and the morphology of the region. Continued on page 73

COULTERVILLE

Rich in history, Coulterville has a warmhearted liveliness not commonly found today. The people here are very proud of their little town and don't mind saying so. Here you will find a store, a museum, a couple of restaurants, hotels, and much more. Good camping is available just west of town on Lake McClure. There are other "unfancy" historic towns nearby. Hornitos and Bear Valley traversed by Route #24 each has an interesting tale to tell. Based in Coulterville, the adventurous cyclist will thoroughly enjoy these miles of lonely roadways in the hills of western Mariposa and Tuolumne County.

23 GREELEY HILL _____

Starting Point: *Coulterville*
Distance: *48.9 miles*

Total Climb: *5,420 ft.*
Map: *Pages 66-67*

    I didn't expect to find a friendly little community such as Greeley Hill east of Coulterville. Even though fire did substantial damage here, the area is still very beautiful. The burn was not total and many trees and scrub remain unscathed. Areas of tall pines, vast pastures and old barns are separated by burn areas on both sides of Smith Station Road. Grazing cows are about the only traffic in the steep grass- and oak-covered hills northwest of Coulterville.

    In front of the old store in Coulterville, climb northeast through town on Priest Coulterville Road (J20) to the eastern turn on narrow-shouldered Greeley Hill Road. Descend into Greeley Hill, where there is a cafe and store open seven days. Continue over pine-shaded rolling hills, with intermittent burn areas, turning north on Smith Station Road (still J20) a couple of miles later. Smith Station Road traverses more easy tree-shaded and partially burned hills before reaching Highway 120 four miles below Buck Meadows.

    You may get on the new highway now or stay with the old highway for awhile. Roll into Groveland with its classic narrow Main Street, which was never intended to handle the flow of traffic it now does. Stay on Highway 120 all the way down to the south turn on Highway 49 at the Moccasin fish hatchery, which is open to the public. Opposite the Reservoir, take Marshes Flat Road up, up, up, to the summit and the first of ten cattle-guards which follow on the descent. There's an eleventh cattle-guard at a crest, where you turn east on Azucena Court, or Blanchard Road, I think. The sign was bent. In any event, it's the first turn (left) just past the eleventh cattle-guard. These next few turns through scattered homes and Digger pine are confusing. Pass three small dead-end streets before turning south (right) on Chicharra Way. Take the next turn southwest (right) on Chapulin Way, pass one more road then at the stop sign turn east (left) on Granite Springs Road. A half mile later, veer east (left) at the fork on Penon Blanco Road. Pass a turkey farm and some houses before the steep climb on Grade Three pavement to an abrupt summit. Cross the sharp ridge and descend, again steeply, down to Highway 49. Turn south here and roll into Coulterville. If the Marshes Flat climb looks like too much, try returning via either Highway 49 or lonely Priest Coulterville Road.

Marshes Flat Road, looking north. *Continued from page 71*

Motor homes in the park seem to travel in packs, usually following the biggest one; it's probably their spiritual chief, or something. White Wolf, a cool, forested campground just above 8,000 feet, also has a quaint store and cafe open during the summer. Crest at Olmsted Point for magnificant views of Half Dome to the south and Clouds Rest above Tenaya Lake, with magnificant camping, to the east. Tuolumne Meadows, 9 miles beyond Olmsted Point, is a very popular destination, with a visitor center, a mountaineering school ("Go Climb a Rock") and a small store. Campgrounds and trailheads can be found here and horseback riding is also available. What a great idea; new saddlesores. Tioga Pass, surrounded by 12,000 foot peaks, is about seven miles ahead through sublime alpine meadows, past tumbling creeks and windswept granite domes. At 9,941 feet Tioga Pass is enthralling. It will probably leave you short of breath. The region around timberline is one of the most beautiful places on earth. Stark leaning toward barren, yet pure and simple. Life here is very difficult and summer growing seasons only last a few weeks. Snow seldom relinquishes its icy grip from the peaks above 12,000 feet, which are numerous from Yosemite southward. Leave the Park here and pass small lakes, or tarns, lush meadows and weather-worn foxtail pines. Regroup at the store and cafe near Ellery Lake before the 2,760 foot flight down to Lee Vining and Highway 395.

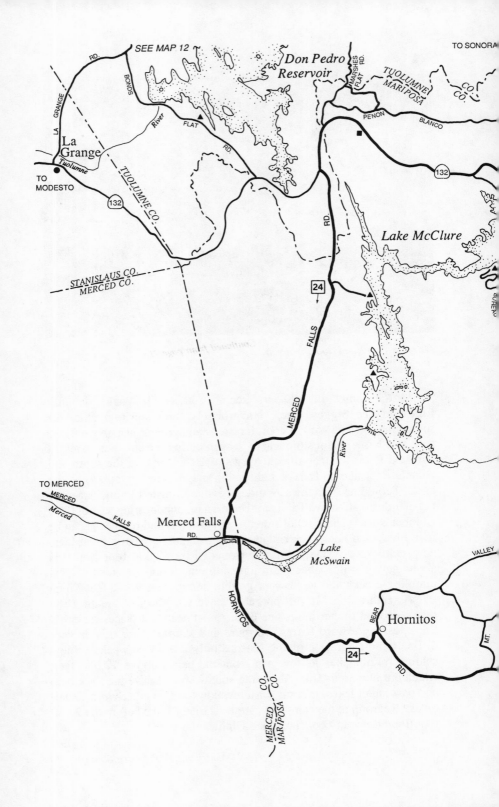

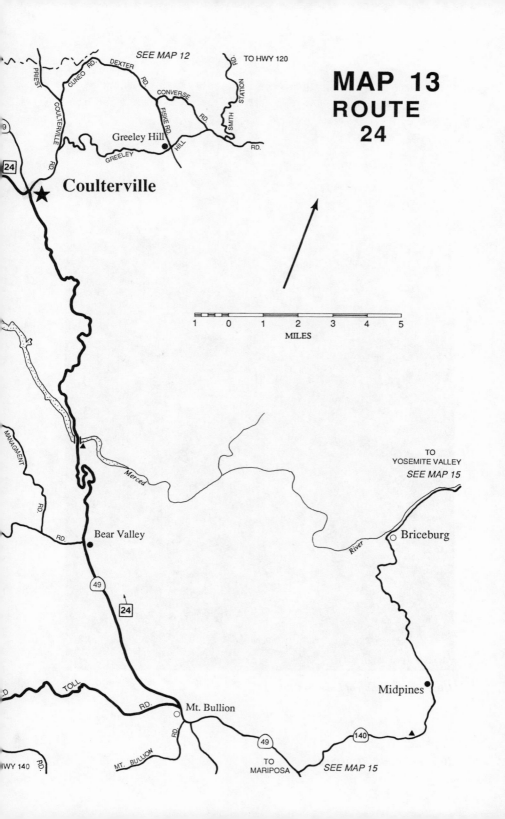

SEE MAP 12

TO HWY 120

PRIEST RD.

CUNEO RD.

DEXTER RD.

CONVERSE RD.

COULTERVILLE RD.

FISKE RD.

SMITH STATION RD.

9

Greeley Hill

GREELEY HILL RD.

24

★ **Coulterville**

**MAP 13
ROUTE
24**

1 0 1 2 3 4 5
MILES

MANAGMENT RD.

Merced

TO
YOSEMITE VALLEY
SEE MAP 15

Bear Valley

River

○ Briceburg

49

24

TOLL

RD.

Midpines

○ Mt. Bullion

RD.

MT. BULLION RD.

49

HWY 140 RD.

TO
MARIPOSA

140

SEE MAP 15

Highway 49, south of Lake McClure.

24 HORNITOS

Starting Point: *Coulterville*
Distance: *64.6 miles*

Total Climb: *5,050 ft.*
Map: *Pages 74-75*

By most accounts Hornitos was the most rootin'-tootin' town west of the Pecos. I hate to disappoint all you party cyclists, but the feds shut it down just last week. You shoulda' been there. Nuthin' but ruins now. Even the cemetery sprouted weeds. That reminds me, Hornitos means "little ovens" in Spanish, supposedly in reference to the oven-shaped above-ground graves built to entomb early inhabitants. But I heard from a very reliable source that Hornitos was actually producing Mrs. Fields cookie clones by the millions. They say they weren't half bad either.

From downtown Coulterville, go west on Highway 132 towards La Grange. After a series of short climbs and descents the road crosses into Tuolumne County and travels south. Just over a mile later, veer southeast on Merced Falls Road toward Lake McClure. A smooth Grade One road rolls through wide open country. Very delightful. Leave Merced Falls Road by swinging east on Hornitos Road (J16), which soon veers south, crosses a bridge over the Merced River, and continues through more enjoyable gently rolling, grassy hills before the relics of Hornitos and those ovens come into view. Swing into "town" and stop for water at the little park. The remains of the store operated by Ghirardelli (you know what they make) can be seen here too.

Continue east-bound on Hornitos Road for six miles and watch for the northeast turn (looks straight) on Old Toll Road where the sign says "to Mount Bullion." Five miles of decent Grade Three road take you through the hills, into forested draws, across small creeks and out to Highway 49. A bar is the only thing in Mount Bullion, so turn north on Highway 49 and head for Bear Valley where the old store is open seven days a week. About a mile later pull over and see the long winding descent into the canyon and the bridge 1320 feet below. If you really squint, you can see the 1420 foot climb out the other side too. It can get toasty on the south-facing hillside, so be sure to have plenty of water on board. Less than five miles lie between you and a nice dinner in Coulterville.

YOSEMITE

Superlatives fall short when describing Yosemite. This is a place that must be experienced first hand and on her own terms. Unfortunately, most visitors here don't venture far from their cars and campsites. They don't see the real valley, away from the noise and crowds. The best way to know Yosemite is to travel on foot, where nothing but trees, granite, and water fill the senses. Leisurely paths wander through quiet forests and beside lush meadows. It's slow, peaceful, and rewarding. The bicycle is also a good way to see some parts of the valley and other less traveled roads that exist within park boundaries ready for cyclists to explore.

Yosemite in the spring is an emotional display of water. It comes gushing and spraying off the granite walls and into the Merced River swollen to twice its normal size. Flowers and meadows burst with life. An organized bike rally is held every spring in the valley, too. Summer is a busy time in the valley; campsites filled, rooms booked, buses packed. The fall is my favorite season in the park; crisp, colorful, in repose. Winter finds the valley quiet, as few people come to see her sleeping under a thin blanket of snow and ice.

Map #16 of the valley floor is provided to show the detailed bikepaths and roads closed to car traffic. There are sufficient miles available to satisfy the leisurely cyclist. The one-way roads in the west end of the valley however, though magnificant in their scenery, are very busy and shoulderless throughout. Don't expect to have the towering granite cliffs, lush meadows, crystaline river, and roadways to yourself. Rental bikes (single speed with baloon tires) are available in Curry Village and at Yosemite Lodge. The roads and paths in the valley are almost totally flat except for a small climb on the road to Mirror Lake.

Merced River and El Capitan.

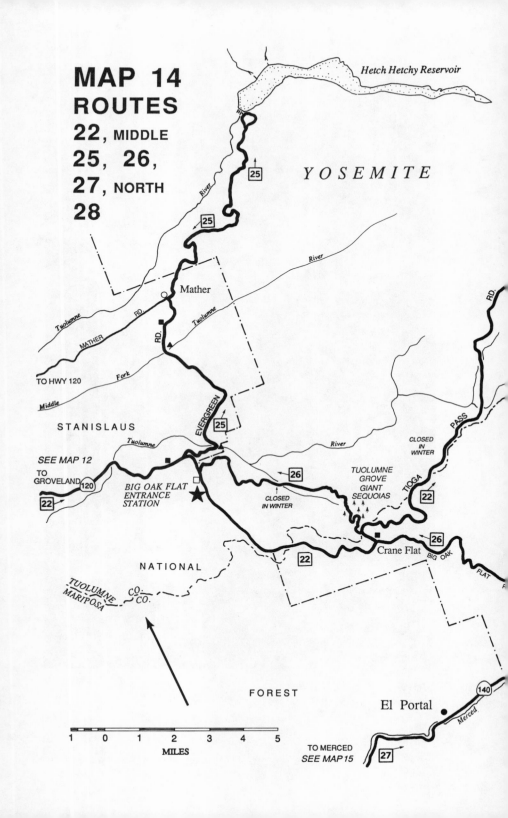

MAP 14
ROUTES
22, MIDDLE
25, 26,
27, NORTH
28

Hetch Hetchy Reservoir

YOSEMITE

River

25

25

River

Mather

Tuolumne

RD.

MATHER   RD.

Tuolumne

Fork

TO HWY 120

Middle

RD.

STANISLAUS

Tuolumne

SEE MAP 12
TO
GROVELAND

EVERGREEN

25

River

CLOSED
IN
WINTER

TIOGA   PASS   RD.

22

120

22

BIG OAK FLAT
ENTRANCE
STATION

26

CLOSED
IN WINTER

TUOLUMNE
GROVE
GIANT
SEQUOIAS

22

26

Crane Flat

BIG OAK

FLAT   R

NATIONAL

22

TUOLUMNE
MARIPOSA

CO.
CO.

FOREST

140

El Portal

Merced

1   0   1   2   3   4   5
MILES

TO MERCED
SEE MAP 15

27

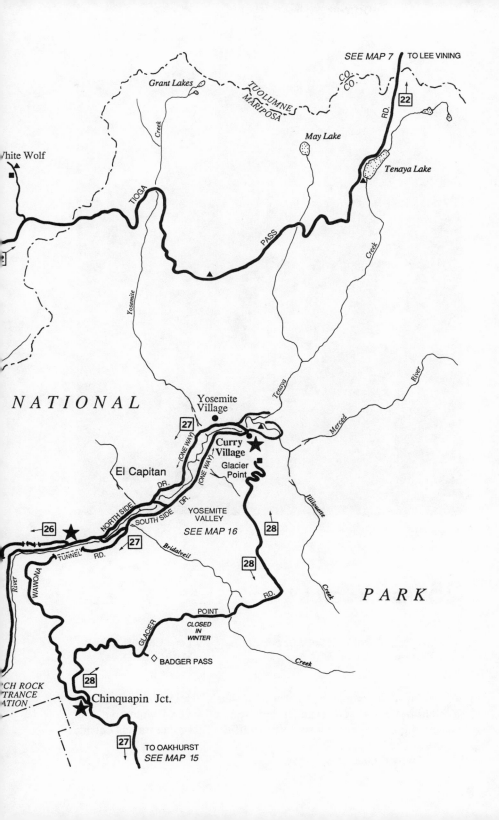

SEE MAP 7 TO LEE VINING

Grant Lakes

TUOLUMNE

MARIPOSA

CO.
CO.

May Lake

22

White Wolf

Tenaya Lake

TIOGA

PASS

Yosemite

Creek

Creek

River

N A T I O N A L

Yosemite
Village

Tenaya

Merced

27

Curry
Village

El Capitan

Glacier
Point

(ONE WAY)

(ONE WAY)

Illilouette

DR.

26

NORTH SIDE

SOUTH SIDE

DR.

YOSEMITE
VALLEY

SEE MAP 16

28

P A R K

27

TUNNEL

RD.

WAWONA

Bridalveil

28

River

GLACIER

POINT

*CLOSED
IN
WINTER*

RD.

Creek

Creek

◇ BADGER PASS

CH ROCK
TRANCE
ATION

28

Chinquapin Jct.

27

TO OAKHURST
SEE MAP 15

Hetch Hetchy Reservoir.

25 HETCH HETCHY

Starting Point: *Big Oak Flat Ent. Stn.* **Total Climb:** *1,230 ft.*
Distance: *35.2 miles* **Map:** *Pages 80-81*

John Muir compared the beauty of Hetch Hetchy Valley to that of
Yosemite Valley. Now under hundreds of feet of water but still
enchanting, Hetch Hetchy sees little traffic. This route travels outside

the park boundary then re-enters near Mather. Two of the three forks of the Tuolumne River are crossed on the 17.6 mile journey to O'Shaughnessy Dam. Views into the depths of the Tuolumne River canyon and Poopenaut Valley are spectacular. I highly prefer this lightly-traveled route over the roads in the crowded valley, especially on busy weekends.

From the Big Oak Flat Entrance Station, descend west-bound on Highway 120 about a mile to Evergreen Road and turn east. Continue the descent to the bridge on the Tuolumne River and climb out. A small section of burned area exists here too, but is being cleared of trees. The lightly traveled pine- and fir-shaded road skirts meadows and crosses creeks and rivers before reaching the delightful little store and cabins at Evergreen Lodge. Turn east on Hetch Hetchy Road at Mather Camp and re-enter Yosemite Park less than a mile later. Cool forest and warm exposed hillside are toured before the first view of the reservoir at a crest. Enjoy the descent along the north facing slope overlooking the river far below. Stop at the Ranger Station for a cool drink of water and restrooms if you need them. Continue around the one-way loop down to the impressive O'Shaughnessy Dam. It was built by San Francisco to supply water to a city rebuilding from the 1906 quake and fire. But the price paid to secure water in this magnificent granite valley was a very high price indeed. Some impressive falls can be seen from the dam, or from the trail that begins on the north side. Return by following the loop back to Hetch Hetchy Road then southwest through Mather and back to Highway 120.

26 TUOLUMNE GROVE

Starting Point: *Yosemite Valley* **Total Climb:** *2,780 ft.*
Distance: *16.7 miles* **Map:** *Pages 80-81*

The purpose of this route is two-fold. The first portion shows the climb from the valley at Highway 140, through three tunnels and out to Crane Flat. Because this is the main access into the valley, many cyclists will enter or leave the valley this way. I do not recommend this very narrow and treacherous portion for leisurely cycling, however. The second portion descends on a one-way road through the Tuolumne Grove of giant Sequoias. This route makes a good day ride, especially when combined with Route #25. If you start at Crane Flat you must return via Highway 120, or plan a car shuttle.

From the small lot in Yosemite Valley where Big Oak Flat Road leaves Highway 140, ascend the narrow road and enter the first short tunnel after one mile. The second tunnel comes a short distance later. The third tunnel is the longest at .4 mile so be very careful here. Crane Flat is only 9.5 miles from the valley and the store there is open every day.

The entrance to Tuolumne Grove is due north of Crane Flat near the Ranger Station. This was one of the main roads into Yosemite back in "the good old days" before motor homes. The big trees come into view less than a mile later where an old "drive thru" relic stands silently as smaller cars pass beneath. The road is steep and bumpy but well worth the effort. Beyond the big trees, picnic tables make a good rest spot. A short climb past a campground will deposit you just inside the entrance to the park on Highway 120. Water, restrooms, and visitor information are available here.

27 WAWONA AND EL PORTAL

Starting Point: *Yosemite Valley*
Distance: *120.5 miles*

Total Climb: *9,740 ft.*
Map: *Pages 80-81, 86-87*

I would be very surprised and very impressed by anyone who rides this, the longest route, completely around. Even though the scenery is incredible and varied, the climbs challenging and the descents thrilling, the distances are quite long. The main purpose in presenting it is to show the western end of Yosemite Valley, the south and central access routes to the valley, and also the southern end of Highway 49 at Oakhurst. Killing four birds with one stone, you might say. As far as cycling is concerned, El Portal, the central entrance, has the easiest grade but can get rather toasty on summer afternoons. The only part of the route with any shoulder is the 18 mile Mariposa County portion of Highway 49 and Highway 140 to Briceburg. Both of the one way roads in the west end of the valley are beautiful and open to cyclists, but are very hazardous in my opinion. Narrow shoulderless roads and tourists looking for waterfalls and bears give me chills.

Old Big Oak Flat Road through giant sequoias.

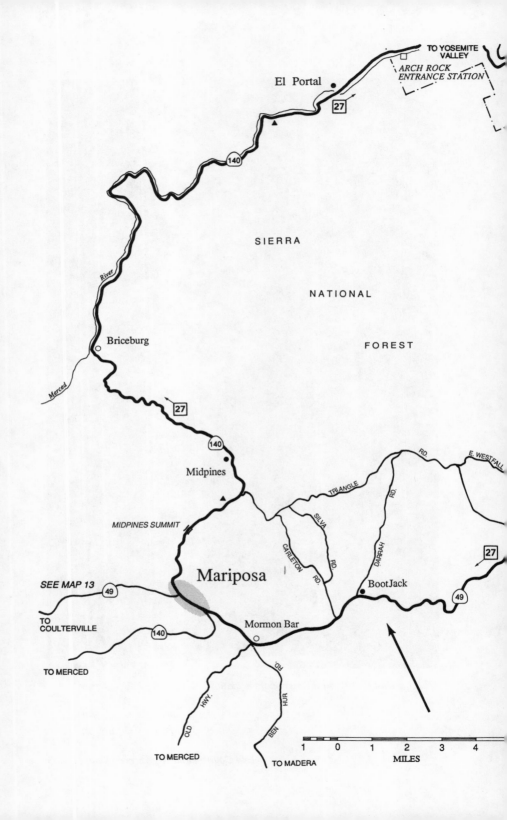

MAP 15 ROUTE 27, SOUTH

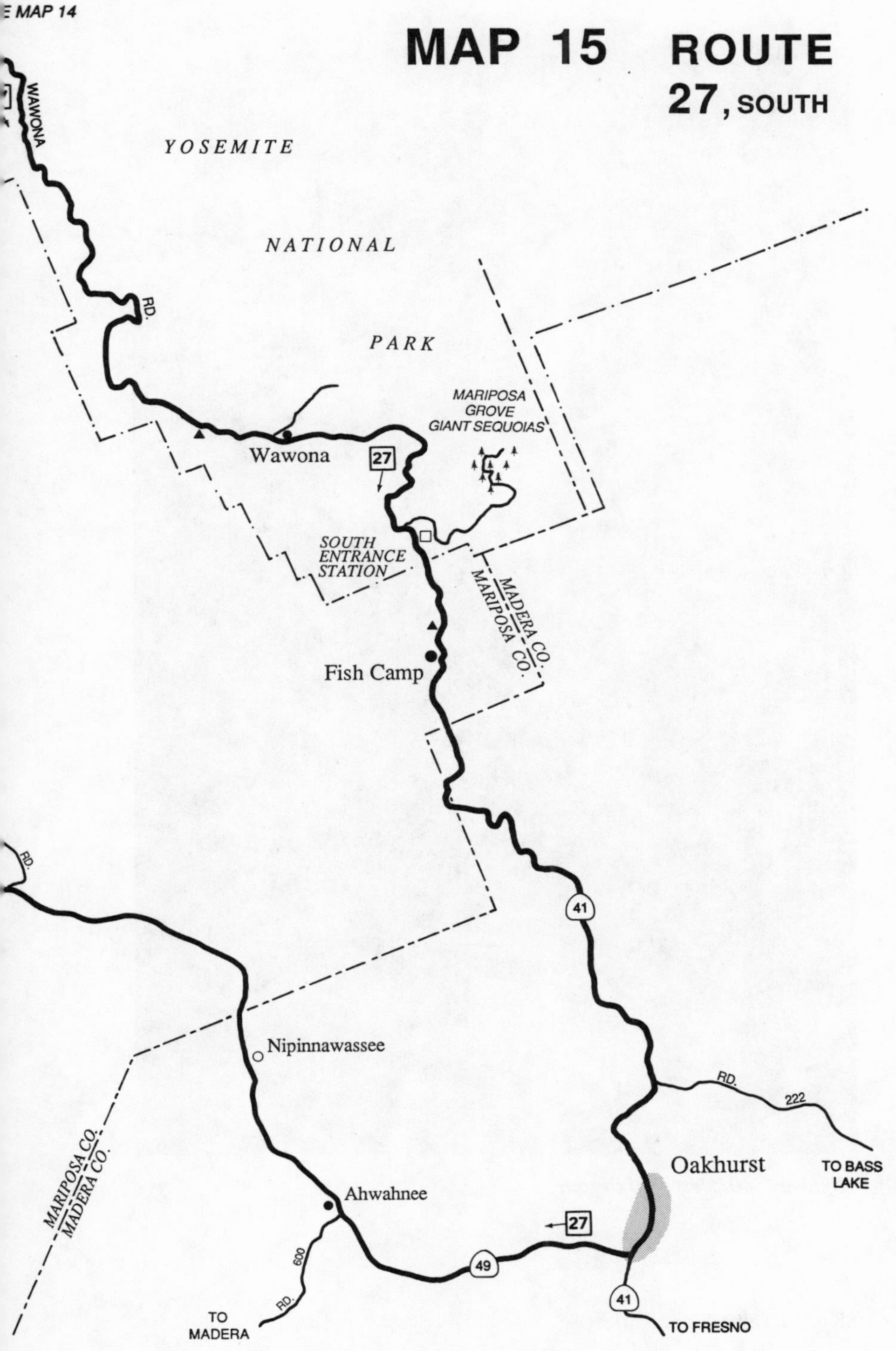

E MAP 14
WAWONA
RD.
YOSEMITE
NATIONAL
PARK
MARIPOSA
GROVE
GIANT SEQUOIAS
Wawona
27
SOUTH
ENTRANCE
STATION
MADERA CO.
MARIPOSA CO.
Fish Camp
41
RD.
Nipinnawassee
RD.
222
TO BASS
LAKE
Oakhurst
MARIPOSA CO.
MADERA CO.
Ahwahnee
27
600
RD.
49
41
TO
MADERA
TO FRESNO

Highway 140, west of El Portal.

From the Curry Village parking lot, take South Side Drive west a quarter mile to North Side Drive and turn north to cross the Stoneman Bridge. Stay with North Side over six miles to the south turn where the sign says "to Hwy 41 and Fresno." Cross the Pohono Bridge, then turn west on Wawona Road and climb steadily up to the Wawona Tunnel. This .8 mile long tunnel is dark and hazardous; be careful. Crest out just beyond the Glacier Point Road (see Route #28) and descend into Wawona. A campground, store, gas station, hotel and golf course are found here. Climb out to the south entrance and over to Fish Camp. Next comes a marvelous 14 mile descent through cool pine and cedar before you reach the warm foothills and Oakhurst below. Here at the southern extremity of Highway 49, Oakhurst is not typical of Gold Country settlements to the north. Built with permanence in mind and not a temporary camp that just happend to survive, the streets are wide and the houses are situated throughout the area. Though not many historical sites remain, plenty of eating places exist here to fuel the hungry cyclist.

Turn onto the southern end of Highway 49 and head north. Cross many small pine-shaded summits and pass a few sleepy towns among the warm grass- and oak-covered hills before rolling into lively Mariposa. This picturesque town at the foot of the Sierra, which has food, lodging, and a good museum, is the last settlement of any size before you return to Yosemite. Just out of town, continue north, now on Highway 140, and cross Midpines Summit. Briceburg is only a wide spot in the road, but the cool Merced River is a welcome sight. Follow the river, pass two campgrounds and maybe stop for a swim, before arriving at El Portal. Spanish for "a gateway" El Portal is the gateway to Yosemite and is at the terminus of the Yosemite Railroad. A small collection of locomotives can be seen here. A low stone wall along the road leaves no shoulder through the Arch Rock entrance and into the park, so be very careful here. Turn south and cross the Pohono Bridge again before the final turn east on South Side Drive, which returns you to Curry Village where you began.

MAP 16
ROUTE
27, 28,
YOSEMITE VALLEY
DETAIL

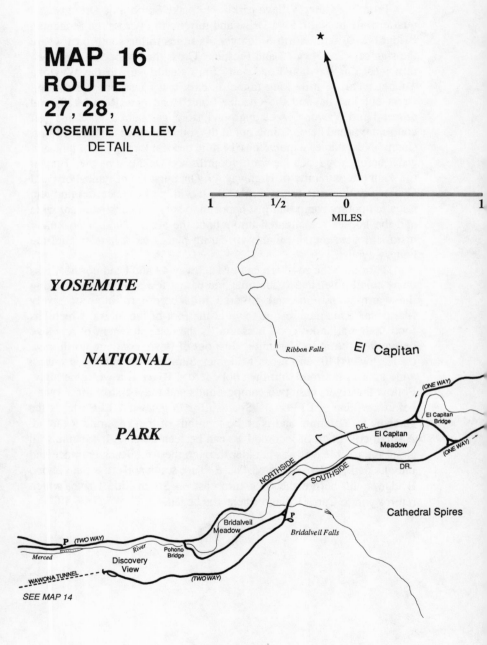

1   1/2   0   1

MILES

YOSEMITE

NATIONAL

PARK

Ribbon Falls

El Capitan

(ONE WAY)

El Capitan
Bridge

DR.

El Capitan
Meadow

(ONE WAY)

NORTHSIDE

SOUTHSIDE

DR.

Cathedral Spires

Bridalveil
Meadow

P

Bridalveil Falls

P (TWO WAY)

River

Pohono
Bridge

Merced

Discovery
View

WAWONA TUNNEL

(TWO WAY)

SEE MAP 14

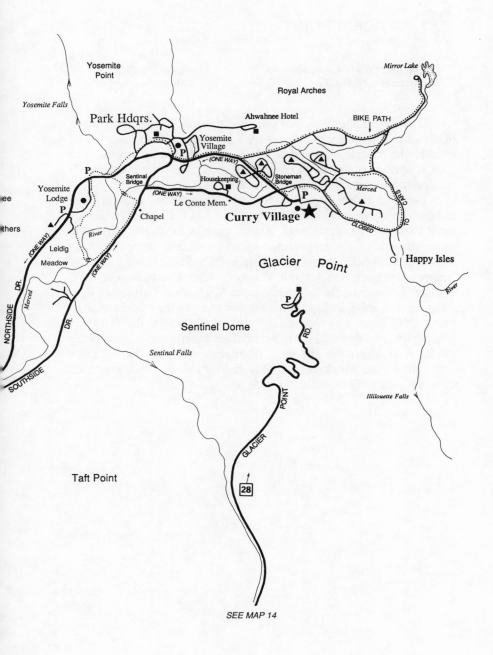

Yosemite
Point

Yosemite Falls

Park Hdqrs.

Royal Arches

Ahwahnee Hotel

BIKE PATH

Mirror Lake

Yosemite
Village

P

(ONE WAY)

Sentinal
Bridge

Housekeeping

Stoneman
Bridge

Yosemite
Lodge

P

(ONE WAY)

Le Conte Mem.

P

Merced

Curry Village ★

Chapel

River

Leidig
Meadow

Merced

(ONE WAY)

Glacier   Point

Happy Isles

River

NORTHSIDE   DR.

SOUTHSIDE   DR.

Sentinel Dome

Sentinal Falls

P

RD.

Illilouette Falls

Taft Point

GLACIER   POINT

28

CLOSED

TO CARS

SEE MAP 14

28 GLACIER POINT _____

Starting Point: *Chinquapin Jct.*　　　　**Total Climb:** *2,320 ft.*
Distance: *31.6 miles*　　　　　　　　　**Map:** *Pages 80-81*

　　If you were allowed to see only one thing in Yosemite the views of the valley from the top of this shear 3,200 foot wall of granite would probably be enough. Arriving by bike can only add to the reward. The road is narrow and steep in places, but these aren't the things you'll remember after returning from Glacier Point.

　　Begin at the small parking lot at Chinquapin on Wawona Road but be sure to arrive with full water bottles and fuel. Ascend Glacier Point Road past pleasant-smelling chinquapin, a shrub, then around to the north side of the mountain, which is cool and shaded by huge mossy pine and fir. Pass the Badger Pass Ski Resort, closed in summer, and crest into Summit Meadow. After a nice descent, cross Bridalveil Creek shortly before it plunges 620 feet over Bridalveil Falls down in Yosemite Valley. Climb again and catch glimpses of Half Dome and Clouds Rest through the trees. A little dip to the Taft Point parking lot is followed by a steep drop through tight corners and out to the large lot above the gift shop, restrooms, and snack bar. Calmly walk out to the overlook and soak it in. I don't think you need direction back to Chinquapin, do you?

Half Dome and Clouds Rest.

APPENDICES

PROFILES

Profiles are a useful method of describing the topography of a route and showing distances between points. They are also useful for bragging to your friends and striking terror in the hearts of novice cyclists. But before this fear paralyzes you, please take a close look at one of the profiles and try to visualize how many feet are being gained and over what distance. Those awful-looking shaded areas appear on stretches at least a half mile long in which the elevation gain is greater than 300 feet per mile. That's only about 5.7%. Some wheelchair ramps are steeper than that.

Here is an explanation of the format and symbols used.

• The vertical numbers refer to feet above mean sea level, the horizontal numbers to distance in miles. The ratio is 26.4:1. That means those huge mountains on the profiles are enhanced to 26.4 times taller than they really are.

• Labels are located at the point of contact with a small feature such as a road change or town, or in the center of a larger feature such as a city. The symbol (P) means you pass the feature, and (X) means you cross it (a river, for example).

• Shaded areas define climbs and drops over 5.68% (300 feet per mile) and lasting longer than one-half mile. The underlined percent figure denotes a short pitch steeper than 11.36% (600 feet per mile). This does not mean you will need ropes and pitons, however.

• The black dots in the mileage scale indicate where services can be found. A service generally means a grocery store or a convenience-type gas station, but does not include roadside bars.

• The angled labels designate starting and ending points, while the horizontal ones refer to points within the route.

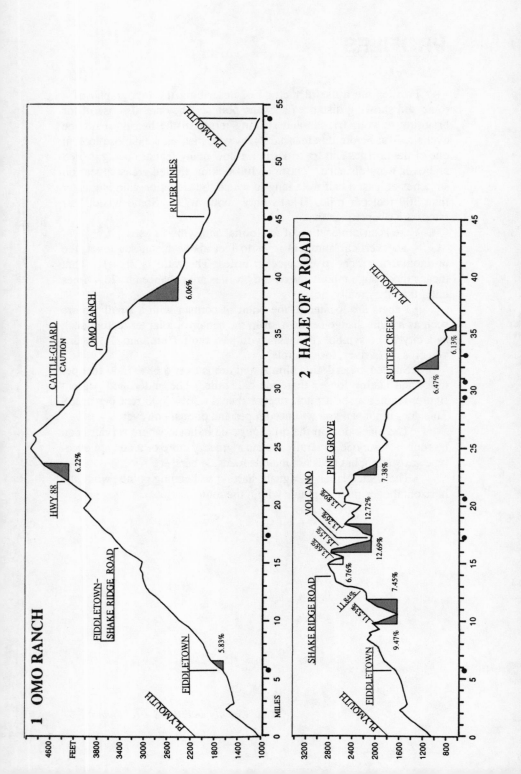

1 OMO RANCH

PLYMOUTH
FIDDLETOWN 5.83%
FIDDLETOWN–SHAKE RIDGE ROAD
HWY 88 6.22%
CATTLE-GUARD CAUTION
OMO RANCH 6.06%
RIVER PINES
PLYMOUTH

2 HALE OF A ROAD

PLYMOUTH
FIDDLETOWN
SHAKE RIDGE ROAD
9.47%
7.45%
11.84%
11.53%
6.76%
12.69%
13.68%
13.15%
13.43%
12.72%
13.89%
VOLCANO
PINE GROVE 7.38%
SUTTER CREEK
6.47%
6.13%
PLYMOUTH

MILES

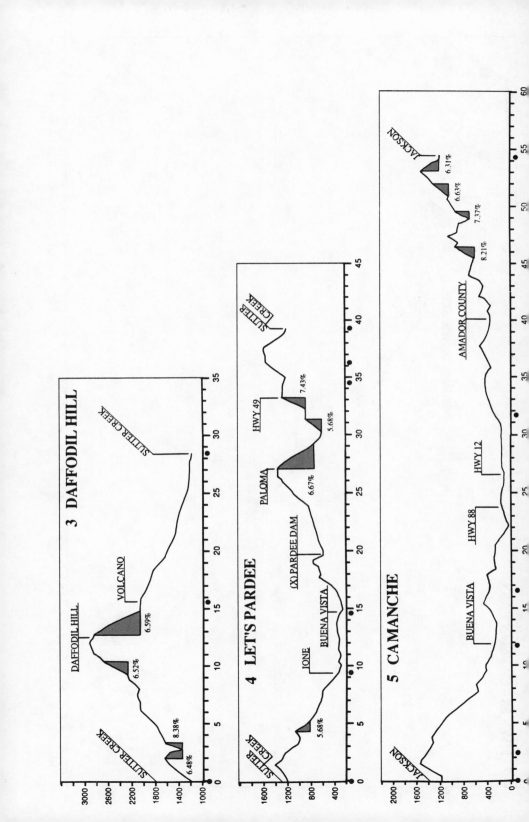

3 DAFFODIL HILL

4 LET'S PARDEE

5 CAMANCHE

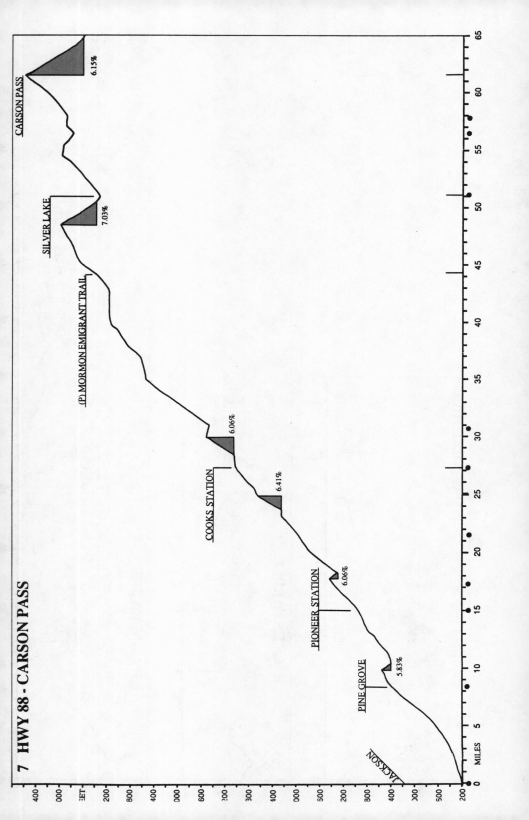

7 HWY 88 - CARSON PASS

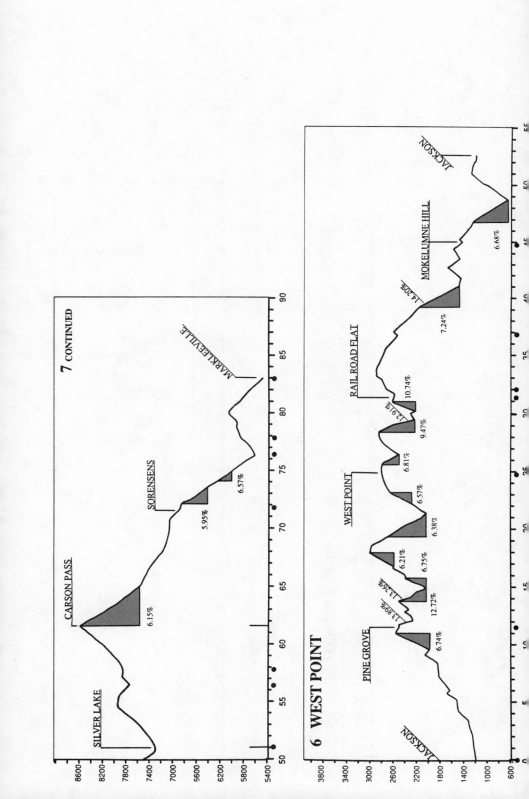

7 CONTINUED

SILVER LAKE

CARSON PASS

6.15%

SORENSENS

5.95%

6.57%

MARKLEEVILLE

6 WEST POINT

JACKSON

PINE GROVE

6.74%

13.89%

13.26%

12.72%

6.75%

6.21%

WEST POINT

6.38%

6.57%

6.81%

9.47%

12.91%

10.74%

RAIL ROAD FLAT

7.24%

14.20%

MOKELUMNE HILL

6.68%

JACKSON

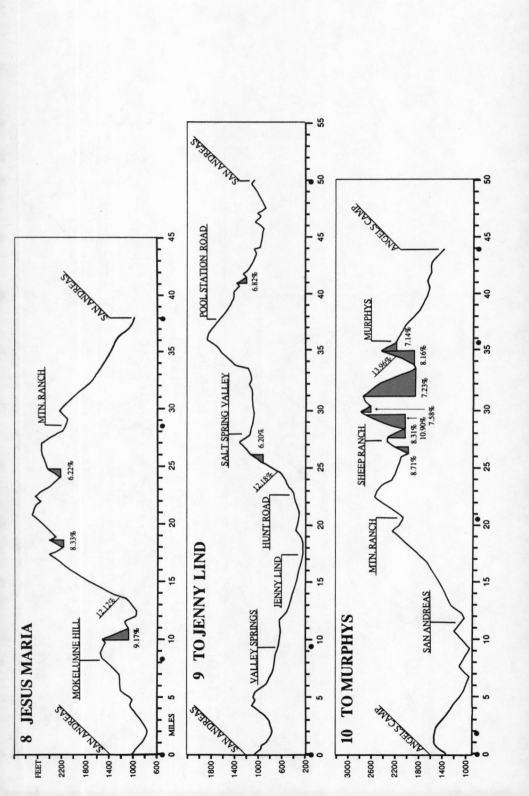

8 JESUS MARIA

SAN ANDREAS · MOKELUMNE HILL · 12.12% · 9.17% · 8.33% · MTN. RANCH · 6.22% · SAN ANDREAS

FEET — 2200 · 1800 · 1400 · 1000 · 600

9 TO JENNY LIND

SAN ANDREAS · VALLEY SPRINGS · JENNY LIND · HUNT ROAD · 12.18% · SALT SPRING VALLEY · 6.20% · POOL STATION ROAD · 6.82% · SAN ANDREAS

1800 · 1400 · 1000 · 600 · 200

MILES · 0 · 5 · 10 · 15 · 20 · 25 · 30 · 35 · 40 · 45 · 50 · 55

10 TO MURPHYS

ANGEL'S CAMP · SAN ANDREAS · MTN. RANCH · SHEEP RANCH · 8.71% · 10.90% · 8.31% · 7.58% · 7.23% · 13.96% · 8.16% · MURPHYS · 7.14% · ANGEL'S CAMP

3000 · 2600 · 2200 · 1800 · 1400 · 1000

0 · 5 · 10 · 15 · 20 · 25 · 30 · 35 · 40 · 45 · 50

11 HWY 4 - EBBETTS PASS

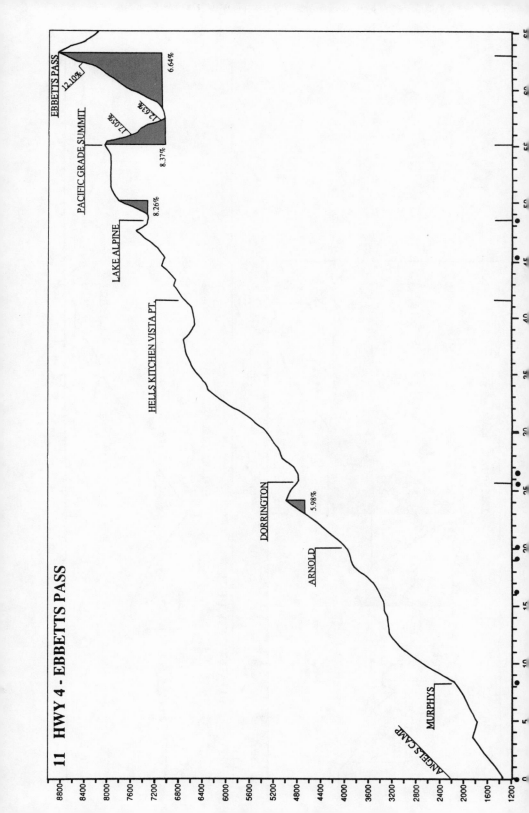

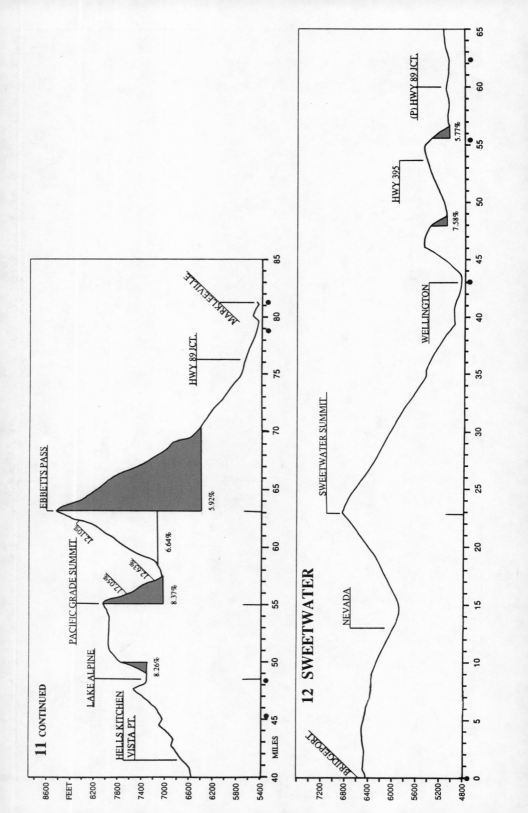

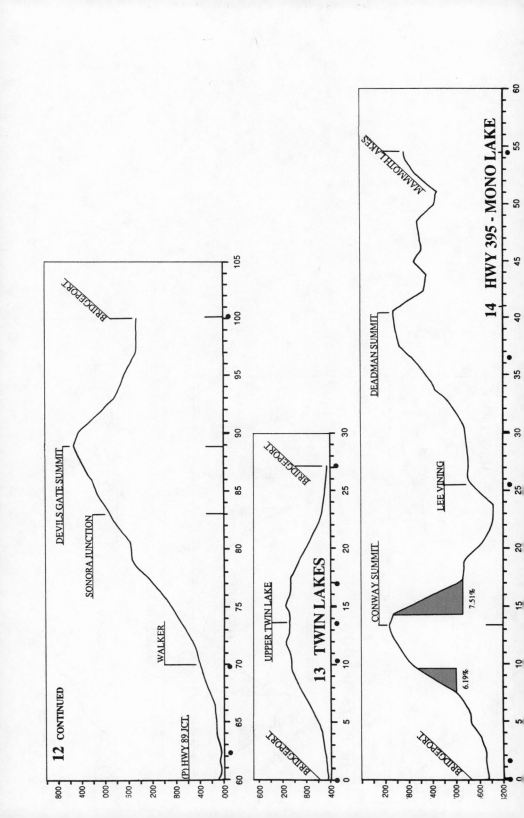

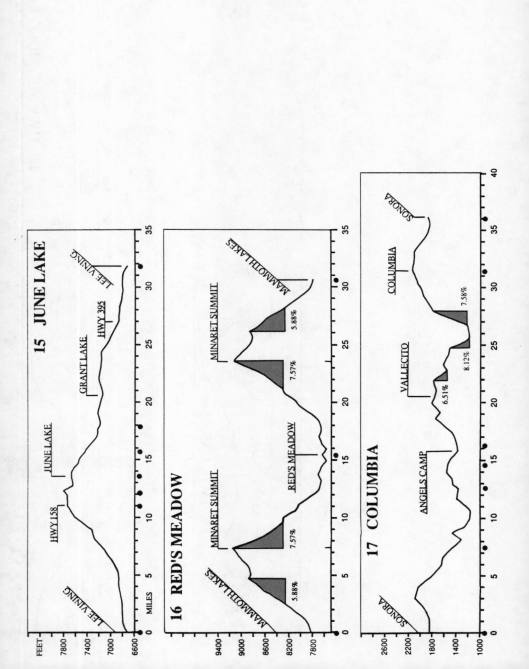

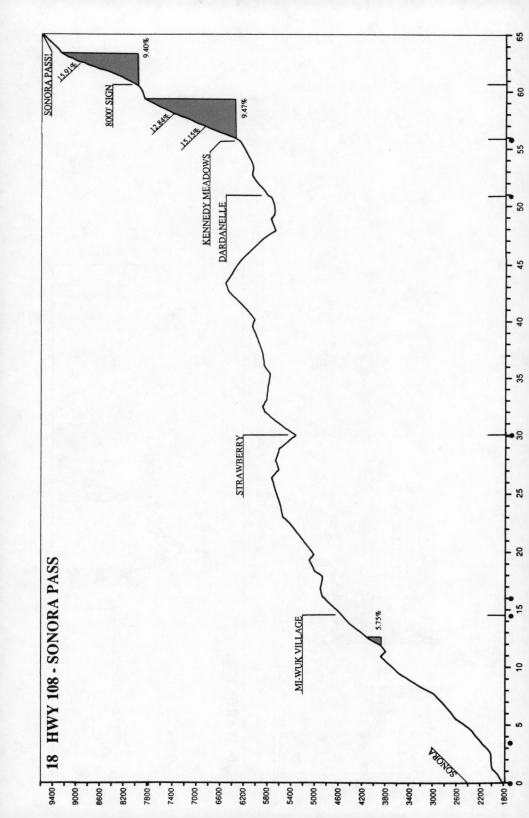

18 HWY 108 - SONORA PASS

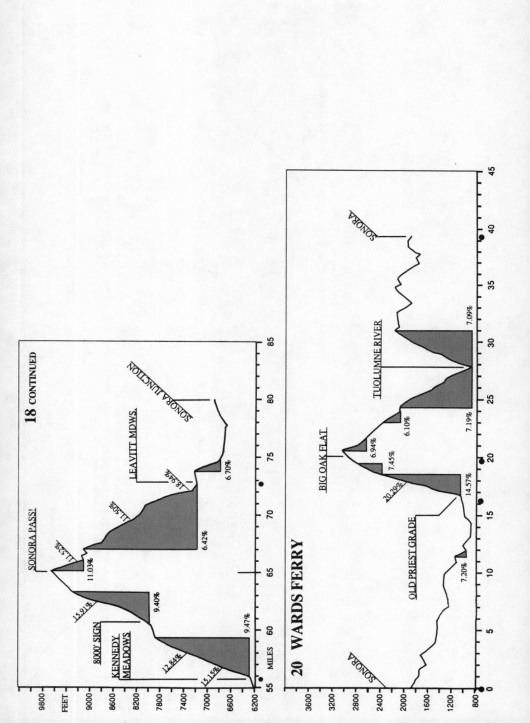

18 CONTINUED

SONORA PASS!

11.52%

11.03%

15.91%

8000' SIGN

KENNEDY MEADOWS

12.84%

15.15%

9.40%

9.47%

11.50%

6.42%

18.94%

LEAVITT MDWS.

6.70%

SONORA JUNCTION

FEET

9800
9400
9000
8600
8200
7800
7400
7000
6600
6200

MILES

55   60   65   70   75   80   85

20 WARDS FERRY

SONORA

OLD PRIEST GRADE

7.20%

14.57%

20.29%

7.45%

6.94%

BIG OAK FLAT

6.10%

7.19%

TUOLUMNE RIVER

7.09%

SONORA

3600
3200
2800
2400
2000
1600
1200
800

0   5   10   15   20   25   30   35   40   45

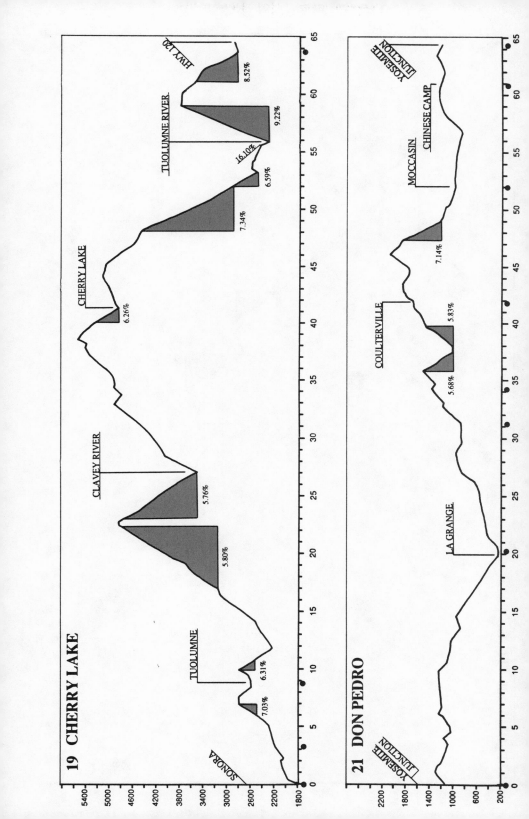

19 CHERRY LAKE

SONORA

TUOLUMNE
7.03%
6.31%

CLAVEY RIVER
5.80%
5.76%

CHERRY LAKE
6.26%

TUOLUMNE RIVER
7.34%
6.59%
16.10%
9.22%

HWY 120
8.52%

21 DON PEDRO

YOSEMITE JUNCTION

LA GRANGE

COULTERVILLE
5.68%
5.83%

MOCCASIN

CHINESE CAMP
7.14%

YOSEMITE JUNCTION

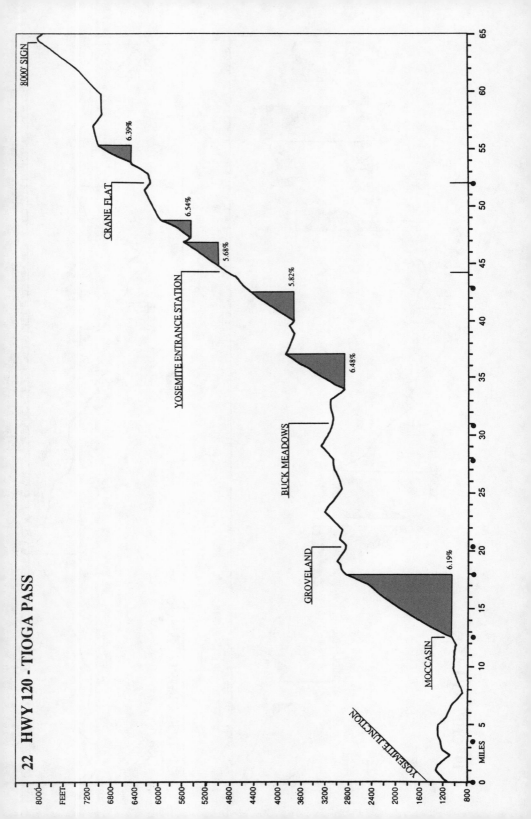

22 HWY 120 - TIOGA PASS

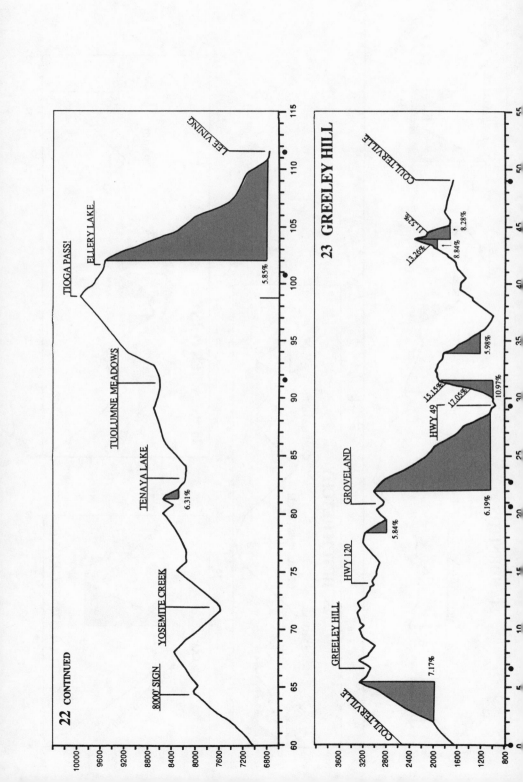

22 CONTINUED

8000' SIGN

YOSEMITE CREEK

TENAYA LAKE

6.31%

TUOLUMNE MEADOWS

TIOGA PASS!

ELLERY LAKE

5.85%

LEE VINING

23 GREELEY HILL

COULTERVILLE

GREELEY HILL

HWY 120

5.84%

GROVELAND

HWY 49

15.15%

17.05%

10.97%

6.19%

5.98%

13.26%

11.52%

8.84%

8.28%

COULTERVILLE

COULTERVILLE

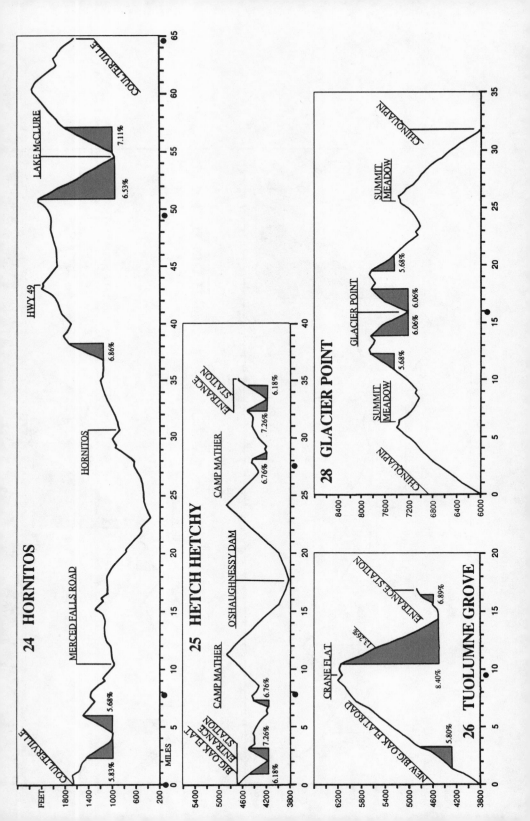

24 HORNITOS

COULTERVILLE · MERCED FALLS ROAD · 5.68% · 5.83% · HORNITOS · 6.86% · HWY 49 · LAKE McCLURE · 6.53% · 7.11% · COULTERVILLE

FEET · 1800 · 1400 · 1000 · 600 · 200

MILES · 0 · 5 · 10 · 15 · 20 · 25 · 30 · 35 · 40 · 45 · 50 · 55 · 60 · 65

25 HETCH HETCHY

BIG OAK FLAT ENTRANCE STATION · 6.18% · 7.26% · CAMP MATHER · 6.76% · O'SHAUGHNESSY DAM · CAMP MATHER · 6.76% · 7.26% · ENTRANCE STATION · 6.18%

5400 · 5000 · 4600 · 4200 · 3800

0 · 5 · 10 · 15 · 20 · 25 · 30 · 35 · 40

26 TUOLUMNE GROVE

NEW BIG OAK FLAT ROAD · 5.80% · CRANE FLAT · 13.26% · 8.40% · ENTRANCE STATION · 6.89%

6200 · 5800 · 5400 · 5000 · 4600 · 4200 · 3800

0 · 5 · 10 · 15 · 20

28 GLACIER POINT

CHINQUAPIN · SUMMIT MEADOW · 5.68% · GLACIER POINT · 6.06% · 6.06% · 5.68% · SUMMIT MEADOW · CHINQUAPIN

8400 · 8000 · 7600 · 7200 · 6800 · 6400 · 6000

0 · 5 · 10 · 15 · 20 · 25 · 30 · 35

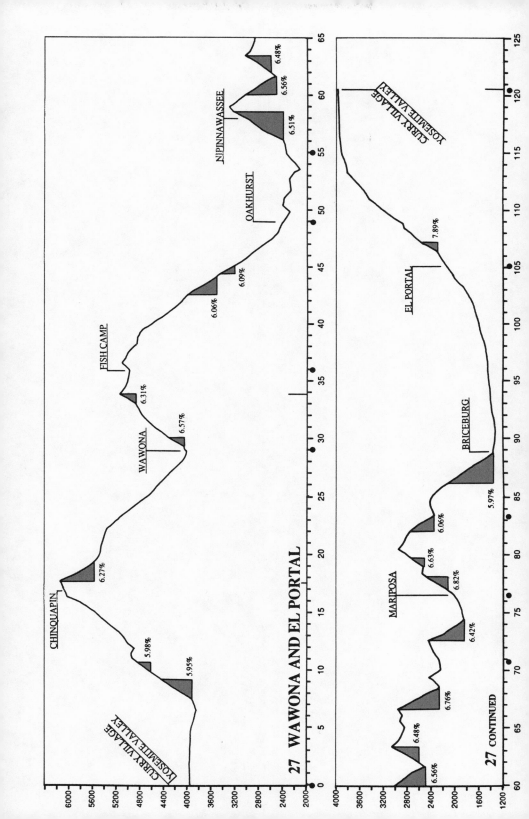

27 WAWONA AND EL PORTAL

27 CONTINUED

WEATHER

Overall, summer in this region is warm and dry, spring and fall are pleasant and mostly dry, and winter is cold and wet. However, this book covers several thousand square miles, extending 100 miles north to south and spanning altitudes from sea level to 9,000 feet. With a range like this you can be sure the weather is diverse and changeable.

The Foothills, a narrow band between the Central Valley and the Gold Country, range in altitude from 100 to approximately 1,000 feet. Winter often finds this area covered by the fringes of the valley fog, which forms between intermittent storms. These storms commonly last one to five days and are separated by about ten days of dry weather. The rains from these storms turn the hills bright green, and the green lasts well into spring when the wet weather comes to an end, usually by early April. Summers are very warm, tending toward hot, as the hills turn golden brown. July and August both average twenty days with temperatures of 90 degrees F. or higher. Record highs have topped 110 degrees F. Summer rain is almost unheard of but can occur in the form of scattered thunderstorms. Wind can be a factor for cyclists in these unprotected hills. The common wind direction is from the west during fair weather and swings south with storm fronts. Fall is warm and dry, with rain beginning in earnest by mid-November. If you live nearby, this area is rideable year-round and will reward you with miles of lonely roads and gentle grades.

The Gold Country has similar weather but lies in a unique zone, often above the winter fog and below the snows. This allows for sunny winter riding between storm fronts. The amount of winter rainfall increases with altitude and latitude. Nevada City averages 54 inches of rain per year while Sonora, to the south and 1,000 feet lower, averages 31 inches per year. Snow is rare and seldom lasts long but does occur. Spring is a great time to cycle here, before the hot weather and summer tourists descend on the area. The hills are green and bursting with wildflowers. Summer weather is delightful too, not as hot as the foothills, and more shady and protected from wind by the trees. Nevada City, for example, averages only fifteen days a month of 90 degree F. or higher temperatures in July and August. Summer thunderstorms are more common as the altitudes increase but are infrequent and short-lived in this area. The terrain is much steeper here, so the sun and the heat can be real hazards if you're not careful. Fall is just spectacular in the Gold Country. The trees are on fire with color, the tourists are less prevalent, and the crisp mornings and warm days make for near-perfect cycling.

Winter finds the High Sierra region above 4,000 feet under a blanket of snow, which increases with the altitude. The record low for the state is 45 degrees F. below zero, recorded near Truckee. It goes without saying that high-altitude cycling isn't too popular during the winter. Springtime is a relative term, relative to the altitude, that is. At the higher passes, for example, sustained springlike temperatures might not occur until June. Tioga Pass is usually open by Memorial Day, but some years has remained closed as late as July 4. The lower and southern portions warm first, as spring reaches into the mountains and brings forth the rush of rivers and blossoms and life. Less than 5% of the total annual precipitation falls during the summer months. Weeks can pass without a cloud, or thunderstorms can bring scattered showers every afternoon for a dozen days in a row.

There is no hard-and-fast schedule for Sierra weather. When riding among the peaks and passes, be sure to prepare for the sun, the cold, and a possible shower, even if there are no clouds in the morning. Wind can be a factor, but direction is nearly impossible to predict with all the peaks and valleys. Up-canyon winds can portend thunderhead buildup. The sun's ultraviolet rays are more intense at higher altitudes, and severe sunburn is a real hazard; be sure to protect exposed skin. Temperatures are usually much cooler the higher you go. The standard rate of cooling is approximately 3 degrees F. per 1,000 feet. If, for example, it's 80 degrees F. in Sacramento (20 feet), it will be approximately 62 degrees F. at Lake Tahoe (6,230 feet), and about 50 degrees F. on Tioga Pass above Yosemite (9,940 feet). This does not take into account localized climates and possible wind-chill factors. It can, and does, get very warm above 8,000 feet. Fall comes early to the High Sierra. The peaks are usually covered by snow before Thanksgiving. The trees bid farewell to summer with a marvelous show of color, especially the black oak, ash, birch, aspen, and cottonwood. This is the time for magnificent solitary travel, before the first snows and after the crowds. Just be prepared for changeable weather.

The East Slope and desert regions covered by this guide range in altitude from 4,000 to 9,000 feet. At the higher altitudes, there is little difference in weather between the High Sierra and East Slope, although the East Slope is more arid and has less runoff due to the rain shadow effect. Even as you descend into the desert, summer highs seldom top 100 degrees F. because of the fairly high altitudes. Thunderstorms are a little more common here. Lightning is the main hazard in the wide open country of the Eastern Slope and deserts. Don't panic though; thunderstorms aren't very good at sneaking up on people quietly. Fall weather is warm, dry, and pleasant. The first cold snap often occurs in October and turns the aspen groves bright yellow. In general, the region east of the Sierra crest is marvelous for cycling and is enhanced by the typically warm, dry weather.

If you want more specific weather information, talk to the National Weather Service, a local chamber of commerce, or a State Park or Forest Service ranger.

SLOPE CONVERSION TABLE _____

This chart allows you to correlate percent slope with feet per mile. For example, if the profile shows a climb at 6.8%, you would be climbing 360 feet per mile. Inversely, if you know how many feet per mile you are climbing, you can easily find the percent slope.

FEET PER MILE	PERCENT SLOPE	FEET PER MILE	PERCENT SLOPE
20	.38	20	11.74
40	.76	40	12.12
60	1.14	60	12.50
80	1.52	80	12.88
100	1.89	700	13.26
20	2.27	20	13.64
40	2.65	40	14.01
60	3.03	60	14.39
80	3.41	80	14.77
200	3.79	800	15.15
20	4.17	20	15.53
40	4.56	40	15.91
60	4.92	60	16.29
80	5.31	80	16.67
300	5.68	900	17.05
20	6.06	20	17.42
40	6.44	40	17.80
60	6.82	60	18.18
80	7.21	80	18.56
400	7.58	1000	18.94
20	7.95	20	19.32
40	8.33	40	19.69
60	8.71	60	20.08
80	9.09	80	20.45
500	9.47	1100	20.83
20	9.85	20	21.21
40	10.23	40	21.61
60	10.61	60	21.97
80	10.98	80	22.35
600	11.36	1200	22.73